AN
ENGLISH
C·H·R·I·S·T·M·A·S

AN
ENGLISH
C·H·R·I·S·T·M·A·S

AN ENGLISH C·H·R·I·S·T·M·A·S

CELIA McINNES

WITH CONTRIBUTIONS FROM
ANGELA FISHBURN · PAMELA WESTLAND
CAROLINE HARRINGTON

HENRY HOLT AND COMPANY

NEW YORK

First published in the United States in 1986 by Henry Holt and Company Inc.,
521 Fifth Avenue, New York, New York 10175.
Originally published in Great Britain under the title *A Christmas Celebration*.
Library of Congress Cataloging-in-Publication Data
McInnes, Celia.
An English Christmas.
British ed. published under title: A Christmas celebration.
Includes index.
1. Christmas—England.   I. Title.
GT4987.44.M36 1986   394.2'68282'0942   86-7553
ISBN 0-8050-0043-7

First American Edition

Special photography by James Jackson and James Murphy
Illustrations by Heather Jane Davies and Oriol Bath

Printed in Singapore by Toppan
Typeset by Bookworm Typesetting, Salford

1 3 5 7 9 10 8 6 4 2

CONTENTS

CHRISTMAS EVE

'Twas the night before Christmas,
When all through the house
Not a creature was stirring,
Not even a mouse;
The stockings were hung
By the chimney with care,
In hopes that St Nicholas
Soon would be there;
The children ere nestled
All snug in their beds,
While visions of sugar-plums
Danced in their heads . . .

From *A Visit from St Nicholas*, by Clement C. Moore

History and TRADITIONS

Here we come a-wassailing
Among the leaves so green,
Here we come a-wandering,
So fair to be seen:

Love and joy come to you,
And to you your wassail too,
And God bless you, and send you
A happy New Year,
And God send you
A happy New Year.

From a traditional North of England *Wassail Song*, anon.

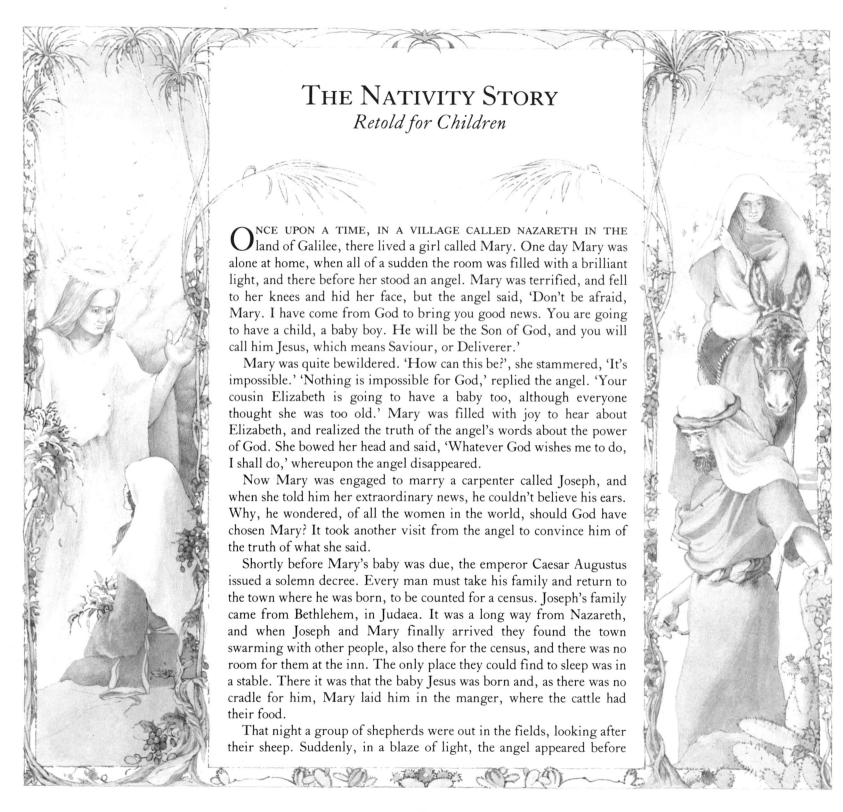

THE NATIVITY STORY
Retold for Children

ONCE UPON A TIME, IN A VILLAGE CALLED NAZARETH IN THE land of Galilee, there lived a girl called Mary. One day Mary was alone at home, when all of a sudden the room was filled with a brilliant light, and there before her stood an angel. Mary was terrified, and fell to her knees and hid her face, but the angel said, 'Don't be afraid, Mary. I have come from God to bring you good news. You are going to have a child, a baby boy. He will be the Son of God, and you will call him Jesus, which means Saviour, or Deliverer.'

Mary was quite bewildered. 'How can this be?', she stammered, 'It's impossible.' 'Nothing is impossible for God,' replied the angel. 'Your cousin Elizabeth is going to have a baby too, although everyone thought she was too old.' Mary was filled with joy to hear about Elizabeth, and realized the truth of the angel's words about the power of God. She bowed her head and said, 'Whatever God wishes me to do, I shall do,' whereupon the angel disappeared.

Now Mary was engaged to marry a carpenter called Joseph, and when she told him her extraordinary news, he couldn't believe his ears. Why, he wondered, of all the women in the world, should God have chosen Mary? It took another visit from the angel to convince him of the truth of what she said.

Shortly before Mary's baby was due, the emperor Caesar Augustus issued a solemn decree. Every man must take his family and return to the town where he was born, to be counted for a census. Joseph's family came from Bethlehem, in Judaea. It was a long way from Nazareth, and when Joseph and Mary finally arrived they found the town swarming with other people, also there for the census, and there was no room for them at the inn. The only place they could find to sleep was in a stable. There it was that the baby Jesus was born and, as there was no cradle for him, Mary laid him in the manger, where the cattle had their food.

That night a group of shepherds were out in the fields, looking after their sheep. Suddenly, in a blaze of light, the angel appeared before

them. Like Mary, they fell to their knees in terror, but the angel said, 'Don't be afraid. You should rejoice and be happy because I've come to bring you some wonderful news. A child was born today whose name is Jesus Christ, and he will be the Saviour of your people. You will find him wrapped in swaddling clothes and lying in a manger.'

As he spoke, a whole host of angels appeared in the sky, singing praise to God and peace to all men. Then, as suddenly as they had come, the angels disappeared, leaving the shepherds speechless with amazement. As soon as they had got over the shock they set off for Bethlehem, taking with them as a present the only precious thing they had to give, a new-born lamb.

Meanwhile a great new star had appeared in the sky. Astrologers said that it signified the birth of a new king, and three wise men from the East set off to search for him, taking with them precious gifts of gold and frankincense and myrrh. They journeyed for many miles following the star, and when they arrived at the city of Jerusalem they stopped to enquire if anyone had heard about the birth of Jesus. Herod, the king, summoned the wise men to him and questioned them very closely. He didn't like the sound of another king in Judaea, and made up his mind to get rid of him. So as the wise men left he said to them, 'When you find this new-born king, let me know where he is, so that I can come and worship him too.' The wise men never suspected that Herod meant the child any harm, but the angel warned them in a dream not to tell Herod where to find Jesus.

So they arrived at the stable in Bethlehem and, like the shepherds before them, knelt before the infant Jesus, joyful but also amazed that in this humble place should be born the King of Kings.

This is what we celebrate at Christmas time – that day nearly two thousand years ago when Jesus Christ came into the world, with only a humble manger for a cradle.

PAGAN ORIGINS

MANY OF THE CHRISTMAS CUSTOMS we keep today have their origins thousands of years before Jesus Christ was born, when people worshipped the sun as the giver of life. Pagan customs adopted by Christianity celebrated the end of winter on the shortest day (21st December) and the coming of spring.

The Romans held Saturnalia and Brumalia, the birthday of the unconquered sun, at this time and the rituals that went with these festivals became part of Christianity when it was adopted by the Roman empire in the fourth century.

In the countries of the Norsemen the midwinter festival was Juul, or Yule. In Britain the Druids kept the Festival of Nolagh. In France Noël and in Italy Natale were also pre-Christian in origin, Natale originally referring to the birth of the New Year rather than to that of the Christ child, and indeed in these countries New Year still carries greater importance than Christmas itself.

It is thought that the midwinter festivals 'became' Christmas after the arrival in England of St Augustine at the end of the sixth century. Rather than try to stamp out the pagan customs, the church simply took them over, applying its own meanings to old rituals.

For, surprising as it may be to us now, when 25th December is indissolubly linked with the birth of Jesus, in the early days of Christianity this event was not only not celebrated in any special way but also not fixed as being at any special time of the year. It was only in the fourth century that the church of Western Europe decided on 25th December.

EARLY FESTIVALS AND CUSTOMS

'Janus sits by the fire with double beard,
And drinketh of his bugle horn the wine:
Before him stands the brawn of tusked swine,
And 'Nowel' cryeth every lusty man.'
Geoffrey Chaucer

MEDIEVAL AND ELIZABETHAN CUSTOMS

The Lord of Misrule The king or lord would appoint someone Lord of Misrule, who would lead the company in (often noisy and disorderly) fun and games throughout the Christmas holiday.

Christmas was traditionally a time for playing games, probably the only time for many people, and everyone seems to have taken full advantage of the relaxed atmosphere to enjoy themselves with games of Hide and Seek, Blindman's Buff, Hunt the Slipper and round games such as Hot Cockles.

Christmas was also a time for music-making and dancing, and in court circles plays would be presented. Shakespeare's *Twelfth Night* was first performed before Elizabeth I on 5th January 1601 and its plot reflects the spirit of happy topsy-turvydom represented by the Lord of Misrule.

Mummers Mummers' plays were once performed all over England at Christmas, nearly every village having its own version. The plays usually centred on a fight between a hero, often St George, and a villain, the Turkish Knight or the Dragon, with a Quack Doctor to revive the fallen hero with his magic elixir. This probably symbolized winter killing the crops which spring then brings back to life.

The mummers, usually men, would take their play round all the houses of their area, receiving small amounts of money, fruit or other food in return for their performance. They did not wear

elaborate costumes but did blacken their faces or cover them with masks, or 'visors'; they had to keep their identity secret if the play was to bring good luck.

Carol-singing This custom goes back at least to the thirteenth century in England and was carried out to commemorate the angels who, according to the Gospels, sang 'Gloria in excelsis Deo' on the night of Christ's birth. At first exclusively done by priests and choristers, carol-singing later became more secular in nature and songs about mince pies and ale began to creep in!

The Yule log The Yule log, the biggest log that could be found to fit the fireplace, would be ceremoniously hauled home on Christmas Eve and lit, if possible, with a piece of the Yule log from the previous year. It was important that the log should burn right through Christmas.

Christmas candles, representing the star of Bethlehem, also shared some of the symbolism of the Yule log.

Boar-hunting A popular Christmas sport in the Middle Ages, boar-hunting also has associations with old Norse mytho-

A group of mummers put on a spirited performance. Mummers' plays used to be enacted in most English villages at Christmas time, and usually featured a fight between hero and villain

logy. The boar's head, decorated with rosemary and bay, would have been the centrepiece of the Christmas feast up to the time of Elizabeth I.

Wren-hunting Wren-hunting over Christmas probably originated with the Druids who captured wrens for use in prophecy. It was particularly common in Ireland and Wales.

The Seventeenth and Eighteenth Centuries

During the rule of Oliver Cromwell the Puritans tried to abolish Christmas altogether. Those aspects of Christmas that they did not condemn as pagan they forbade as being popish; not only were feasting and merrymaking forbidden by Act of Parliament in 1652 but there was to be no special church service on Christmas Day – in fact churches were to be kept shut. John Evelyn, the diarist, wrote in 1657 how he and his wife were arrested by soldiers while attending a Christmas service which was being held in secret.

Most of the old customs were revived when Charles II returned to the throne in 1660 and the religious observance of Christmas was renewed. In 1662 Samuel Pepys attended a Christmas Day sermon which exhorted the congregation 'to joy in these publick days of joy, and to hospitality' but it also criticized 'the common jollity of the Court': the notion of Christmas as a time for wholehearted merrymaking seems to have been superseded by something more sober. On this occasion Pepys did return home to eat 'a mess of brave plum-pudding and a roasted pullet for dinner, and I sent for a mince-pie' but he ate alone and this seems to have been the full extent of his Christmas celebrations.

In Scotland this was particularly true; thanks to the strong Puritan element in that country Christmas never really regained its old glory. To this day the Scots keep New Year as their primary festival.

In the eighteenth century Christmas was not regarded as of great importance;

Christmas Through the Years

DECORATING THE CHRISTMAS TREE

even in 1813, when Jane Austen mentioned it in *Pride and Prejudice*, there is no reference to seasonal observances or rituals, although these were undoubtedly still recognized.

The Nineteenth Century

Christmas really returned as a big event in the nineteenth century with the introduction of various new elements of ritual, some of which were introduced by Queen Victoria's consort, Prince Albert, who brought German Christmas customs with him from his native country. The best known of these was of course the Christmas tree, which Prince Albert had erected in Windsor Castle in 1841. Other features which were new at that time and which we now consider 'traditional' were the Christmas greeting card (first marketed in 1846) and the cracker.

Our present-day ideal of Christmas is based on the romantic revival of the Victorians: presents piled under the candle-lit tree, family attendance at church on Christmas morning, plum pudding and turkey for dinner and crackers to go with them, parlour games, present-filled stockings and Christmas cards depicting robins.

This cosy image of the Victorian Christmas is nowhere presented more fully or persuasively than in the works of a writer who loved it, Charles Dickens. Everyone knows his description of the Cratchits' Christmas dinner. Even though they are poor this family in *A Christmas Carol* have a roast goose with sage and onion stuffing and, to follow, 'a pudding, like a speckled cannonball, so hard and firm, blazing in ignited brandy, with holly stuck into the top'.

Here is a homely evening with the Fezziwigs from the same book: 'There were more dances, and there were forfeits, and more dances, and there was cake, and there was negus, and there was a great piece of Cold Roast, and there was a great piece of Cold Boiled, and there were mince-pies, and plenty of beer.'

Prince Albert's contribution to our tradition was described by Dickens in *Household Words* (1850): 'I have been looking on, this evening, at a merry company of children assembled round that pretty German toy, a Christmas Tree. ... It was brilliantly lighted by a multitude of little tapers; and everywhere sparkled and glittered with bright objects.'

It was Dickens again who summed up, in his *Sketches by Boz* in 1836, what we still hope for today from Christmas: 'Christmas time! That man must be a misanthrope indeed, in whose breast something like jovial feeling is not roused – in whose mind some pleasant associations are not awakened – by the recurrence of Christmas. ... A Christmas family-party! We know of nothing in nature more delightful! There seems a magic in the very name of Christmas.'

Carol-singing gained new popularity in the nineteenth century, the singers being known as 'the waits'. Most of the carols popular today were either composed or took on their present form at that time: 'Away in a Manger' and 'We Three Kings' originated in America in the middle of the century.

VISITING CAROL-SINGERS
Carol-singers became a familiar part of the Christmas festivities
in nineteenth-century England and are often shown
grouped around a lantern

WASSAILING

CUSTOMS LONG CONNECTED WITH wassailing spread themselves over the whole Christmas period. When Worcestershire children went a-begging on St Thomas's Day they sang:

Wassail, wassail, through the town,
If you've got any apples, throw them down;
If you've got no apples, money will do;
The jug is white and the ale is brown,
This is the best house in the town.

The expression 'Wassail!', heard often in the past, comes from the Anglo-Saxon toast *Waes-Hail* (Be whole!) to which the proper response was *Drink-Hail*, or Good health!

The wassail bowl, traditionally holding hot spiced ale with apples, was an important element in Christmas customs over several centuries, especially those associated with the New Year. At home, it was usual for the family, or household, to pass the wassail bowl round with the traditional toast while waiting to be first-footed.

Some areas of England celebrated New Year with wassailing processions, sometimes led by two young girls carrying a wassail bowl decorated with ribbons and greenery. The procession would make its way from house to house – this might be on New Year's Eve or New Year's Day – and invite those it visited to drink 'wassail' in honour of the season and then fill up the bowl again. Those too poor to buy ale at all would go 'a-wassailing' in the expectation of having their Wassail Cup filled for them by the better-off households they called on and in the hope of gifts of fruit or money.

TRADITIONAL CELEBRATIONS AND SHOWS

Fruit tree wassailing usually took place at Twelfth Night; it was particularly common in the main fruit-growing counties of Kent and the West of England. Cider was drunk from the wassail bowl then sprinkled on the fruit trees in order to ensure their fertility in the coming year. The men would then fire shotguns into the branches or, in Surrey, whip the trunks of the trees.

Here's to thee, old apple-tree!
Whence thou mayst bud,
Whence thou mayst blow,
And whence thou mayst bear
apples enow!
Hats full!
Caps full!
And my pocket full, too!
Hurrah! Hurrah!

MASQUES

ALTHOUGH NOT CONFINED TO Christmas, masques were often presented as part of the celebrations of the Christmas period in the great houses of the nobility and especially at court. They were not a popular form although they did derive loosely from the old mummers' plays in that 'guises' and masks were worn, and they were referred to in the fourteenth century as 'mummings' or 'guisings'.

By the sixteenth century, however, the name of 'masque' had been adopted for these 'events' which seem often to have been little more than elaborate dressing-up sessions: in 1512 the first Italian-style masque was presented at Henry VIII's court for Twelfth Night, with gentlemen 'appareled in garment long and brode, wrought all in gold, with visers and cappes of gold' appearing to dance with the ladies present.

Masques had become something more than tableaux by the time Ben Jonson, the first poet laureate, wrote his; among them were 'The Masque of Beauty', in 1608 and 'Christmas His Masque', written specially for the Christmas of 1616. Since he co-operated with Inigo Jones, the architect, who designed sets and costumes, they were still magnificent – and expensive – affairs.

Puritan rule under Oliver Cromwell put an end to the court and to its masques and the form never really got started again when Charles II was restored to the throne in 1660. Neither the court nor the nobility could any longer afford the extravagance that the staging of masques demanded.

Pantomime

Pantomime is a much more recent phenomenon, with a very mixed ancestry. On the face of it, there is nothing so uniquely, eccentrically British as a pantomime. But it developed from traditions very un-British indeed – and nothing whatever to do with Christmas. It has gone through several transformations since its commercial beginnings under such pioneers as the actor-manager John Rich in London.

Now primarily a children's show, based, if very loosely sometimes, on traditional children's stories, pantomime began as an entertainment for adults. It can be traced right back to the ancient Roman Saturnalia, the mid-winter feast at which everything was turned topsy-turvy; men dressed up as women and women as men – like the Dame and principal boys of the modern-day panto – and fortunes were reversed, masters becoming slaves and slaves, masters – just as Cinderellas marry princes and poor Jacks make vast fortunes.

A more recent antecedent was the *commedia dell'arte*, the Italian tradition of improvised theatre, which became popular in Britain in the eighteenth century. In 1739 pantomime was described as 'a dramatized tale, the dénouement of which is often a tranformation scene followed by the broad comedy of clown and pantaloon and the dancing of harlequin and columbine'. These are stock characters from the *commedia dell'arte*: Harlequin and Columbine are lovers, and old Pantaloon is the villain of the piece, trying to thwart their romance. But as the century progressed, such traditional plots got mixed up with fairy stories, folk tales, or tales from the *Arabian Nights,* and gradually evolved into the dozen or so familiar stories of the panto repertoire. The traditional figures from the *commedia dell'arte* gradually disappeared, and pantomimes became more as we know them today; they also became an expected part of our Christmas festivities, traditionally starting on Boxing Day.

Pantomime was much affected by the rise of the music hall. The stars of the day – burlesque comedians and music hall artistes – took dreadful liberties with the plot in order to accommodate their own star turns. Nowadays pop stars and television personalities continue this tradition, all turning up in panto, no matter how incongruous their presence.

This, though, is what makes pantomime particularly suitable for a family

Little Red Riding Hood
Illustration by E.K. Johnson
in 'The Graphic'

entertainment. It is a form which, within a traditional framework, can accommodate everybody's party piece, and guarantee that nobody will be left out. The audience has to work almost as hard as the performers, whether it be joining in the songs, assisting in conjuring tricks, hissing the villain and warning the hero ('He's behind you!') or chiming in with well-known repartee.

But whatever changes pantomime has gone through, it still retains serious elements of ancient ritual that link it to our distant past. It is this mixture of topicality and tradition that holds the key to its perennial appeal.

CHRISTMAS CARDS

CHRISTMAS CARDS DO NOT HAVE A long history although Christmas would seem very sad without them now. They became popular just over a hundred years ago, having been put on sale for the first time in 1846.

It was Henry, later Sir Henry, Cole, the first director of the then newly founded Victoria and Albert Museum, who was responsible for having the first-known Christmas card designed, hand-coloured and printed. It showed a cheerful family group flanked by scenes of seasonable good works and bore the inscription 'A Merry Christmas and a Happy New Year to You'. About a thousand copies were sold at a price of one shilling each.

Christmas cards would probably not have been devised at all had it not been for the introduction of the penny post in 1840 and it was another new development, the invention of a cheap colour reproduction process, that enabled prices of cards to be brought within the reach of most people.

By the 1860s the idea of sending cards to friends at Christmas had really caught on and they began to be mentioned in magazines (*Punch*, 1863) and newspapers (*The Times*, 1871).

These first Christmas cards looked more like Valentine or wedding anniversary cards with pretty lace edgings or flowery borders and sentimental subjects, but it was not long before designs appeared that we would find familiar today. Robins have been enduringly popular, appearing on a card for the first time in 1862. They were not

VICTORIAN FAVOURITES

PULLING A CRACKER
AT A CHRISTMAS PARTY
This aspect of the celebrations has long been a favourite, and one which the younger members of the family can hardly wait to begin

only shown looking bright and friendly but also dead: the Victorians seem to have been fond of tear-jerking subjects.

Other perennial favourites originated with the Victorians: snow scenes with people in traditional costume (then eighteenth century, now of course more often nineteenth century), Father Christmas in his sleigh, holly and mistletoe designs and Christmas trees and candles. Nativity scenes, angels and other religious pictures also became and remained popular. Some cards were very elaborate with pop-up pictures and moving parts. Queen Mary had a collection of beautiful and unusual cards, some of them three-dimensional, which are now in the British Museum.

CHRISTMAS CRACKERS

ANOTHER FEATURE OF CHRISTMAS which is not very ancient in Britain is the Christmas cracker. This present-day favourite is thought to have originated in France where, on special occasions, children were given bags of sugared almonds which burst with a bang when pulled in half. It is another Victorian who is credited with bringing the idea to England and elaborating on it to produce what we now know as a cracker.

In about 1840 a London baker and confectioner called Thomas Smith visited Paris. He was very impressed by the French idea of selling *bonbons* (sweets) prettily wrapped in twists of coloured paper. Back at home he produced his own version, including a love message, later a motto or riddle as a sales novelty. When his sweets failed to sell he

An example of the first-known Christmas card, now in the Victoria and Albert Museum. It was commissioned by Sir Henry Cole in the early 1840s and designed by J.C. Horsley

put in the bang (in the form of chemically treated card) and never looked back – by the end of the century his company was producing millions of crackers a year for both home and export sale. It is still in business.

Tom Smith also introduced tiny toys, games and puzzles into his crackers, or 'cosaques' as they were originally known, and made them just about every size. His biggest was 9 metres (30 feet) high.

Today crackers are such an integral part of our Christmas festivities that it is hard to believe they have not always been around. Even when the bang won't go off and we grumble about the quality of the contents we wouldn't be without our Christmas cracker!

CHRISTMAS BELLS

CHRISTMAS BELLS ARE ANOTHER familiar symbol which has its origin in the church. In former times the faithful flock depended on the ringing of the church bells to summon them to worship, to announce a joyful occasion or commemorate an important festival. So did Scrooge discover, in Charles Dickens' *A Christmas Carol*.

He was checked in his transports by the churches ringing out the lustiest peals he had ever heard. Clash, clang, hammer; ding, dong, bell. Bell, dong, ding; hammer, clang, clash! Oh, glorious, glorious! Running to the window, he opened it, and put out his head. No fog, no mist; clear, bright, jovial, stirring, cold ... Golden sunlight; Heavenly sky; sweet fresh air; merry bells. Oh, glorious! ... Christmas Day!

ROBIN REDBREAST

It is said that after Jesus was born Joseph went out to gather fuel for the fire and was gone so long that Mary became anxious that the fire would go out. Suddenly some small brown birds flew in and began to fan the fire with their wings, keeping it alight until Joseph returned.

But Mary saw that they had scorched their breasts and said, 'From now on you will always have a fiery red breast in memory of what you have done for the baby Jesus. People will love you and will call you Robin Redbreast.'

Robins, as shown in Harrison Weir's 'Pictures of Birds', c. 1870

EVERGREENS HAVE ALWAYS SEEMED magical to people living close to nature because they keep their leaves, and even produce fruit and flowers, throughout the winter. When pagan peoples celebrated their midwinter festivals they brought evergreens into their homes to pay homage to the gods who kept life going in this way through the cold dark days of winter. Evergreens meant good luck to the Romans. They would decorate their homes with branches of holly and ivy and give sprigs of them to friends as good luck tokens during the winter feast of Saturnalia.

Most kinds of evergreen plant were used: pine branches gave damp winter rooms a sweet fresh smell; holly is said to have healing properties; ivy and bay represented a spirit of good cheer, and

EVERGREENS

rosemary was popular as the herb of remembrance – Christmas is a time when we remember our friends as well as the birth of Christ.

The way in which the Christian church applied its own symbolism to the evergreens of which the pagan peoples were so fond is exemplified in the case of holly. The church accepted holly as lucky and caused its sharp leaves to become associated with the crown of thorns that Jesus wore at Calvary, holly's red berries representing drops of His blood. In Scandinavia holly is known as the 'Christ-thorn'.

Although this winter greenery became acceptable by taking on new significance and other evergreens such as laurel and box were and still are used in the decoration of churches, there was one plant that the church just could not bring itself to look upon with favour – mistletoe.

Mistletoe was an important element of certain Druid rites in which it was particularly linked with human sacrifice.

Even today you will rarely see it in a church, probably because of this old connection. Its symbolism is frankly pagan: it is said that after the sacrificial rites those attending took home sprigs of the mistletoe to put over their doors to promote fertility indoors and out. The pleasant custom of kissing under the mistletoe may have derived from this belief. It was also credited with the power to bestow peace and harmony: according to Norse legend mistletoe was used to kill the god Balder then sworn never to do harm to anyone again.

Laurel has been credited with the ability to protect and purify and stood for victory and honour, being used for this reason to decorate those achieving distinction in Ancient Rome – whence the expression, 'resting on your laurels'.

CHILDREN GATHERING MISTLETOE
Nineteenth-century illustration

THE TWENTY-FOURTH OF DECEMBER
Illustration by Jessie Macgregor in 'The Graphic'

THE TRADITION OF THE DECORATed Christmas tree – pine, fir or spruce – is not so old. It was Prince Albert who first set the fashion in England by having one set up in Windsor Castle in 1841 for his own family, because he remembered the pleasure this custom had given him as a child.

Prince Albert brought the idea with him from his native Germany where it had been common for centuries. There are references to Christmas trees decorated with flowers of coloured paper and foil, sweets and fruit as far back as 1605 in Strasbourg. An even earlier German story relates how Martin Luther illuminated with candles a fir tree which he brought indoors to remind children of the starlit heavens from which Jesus Christ descended for our sakes.

CHRISTMAS TREES

Whatever its origins, whether pagan or Christian, the custom is certainly Germanic. Legends about the Christmas tree are connected with St Boniface who visited Germany as a missionary in the eighth century. He is said to have come across a sacred oak tree where a human sacrifice was about to take place and to have chopped down the tree, thus saving the child's life. Where the oak had been St Boniface found a young fir tree – growing between its roots or springing up miraculously in its place according to different versions of the legend. St Boniface saw this new life as symbolic of the new faith he was preaching; as such the Christmas tree became connected with Christianity.

Once introduced into England it was not long before the Christmas tree (already popular in America because of German immigrants there) became the central feature of our Christmas decorations. Today we know that Christmas is near when we see the trees alight with shining colour in the windows along the

street – although purists say we should wait until Christmas Eve – and it is a sad moment when we take them down again on Twelfth Night and say goodbye to their sweet smell and unique appeal for another year.

THE GLASTONBURY THORN
Legend says that, after the death of Christ, Joseph of Arimathaea came to Britain to spread the Gospel. Walking in the West of England, he lay down to rest, having first thrust his staff into the ground. When he awoke he found that his staff had taken root and blossomed and the bush *Crataegus monogyna* 'Biflora', known as the Glastonbury thorn, continued to flower every Christmas Day as a sign of the new hope which the birth of Jesus Christ brought to man.

CHRISTMAS EVE
Detail of oil painting by George Bernard O'Neill

HØJBRO PLADS
Detail of oil painting by David Jacobsen

Our familiar Father Christmas has a long and complex ancestry. On the Christian side, to begin with, we have the fourth-century St Nicholas who was Archbishop of Lycia in what is now Turkey. His name is surrounded by numerous legends.

In one story, St Nicholas was staying at an inn when he dreamt that the innkeeper had murdered three visiting boys. When accosted, the innkeeper confessed and St Nicholas brought the boys back to life.

In another story, St Nicholas rescued three girls from the threat of prostitution by giving them each a bag of gold as a dowry so that they might marry instead. In a third, St Nicholas is said to have travelled from his home to deliver baskets of fruit and grain and honey cakes to hungry children in the West. Now every year St Nicholas comes from heaven to bring his gifts to remind people that Christmas is coming.

In deference to these traditions St Nicholas is the patron saint of boys and girls and on the Continent his feast day, 6th December, is remembered by giving presents to children.

In the Netherlands St Nicholas Day is particularly important. Here he is called 'Sinte Klaas' and he arrives wearing his bishop's mitre and robes and accompanied by his servant Black Peter. In Amsterdam he arrives in a ship, supposedly from Spain, then rides a white horse from house to house where he checks on the behaviour of the children before dispensing presents. Black Peter is there to write down who has and who has not been good; those who have been naughty will not get presents unless their

The Story of Father Christmas

FATHER CHRISTMAS
Illustration by Lizzie Mack, 1889
This is every child's dream at Christmas time

parents speak up for them. That night the children put out their clogs in the hope of a present, and leave food for the white horse.

On the pagan side, we find the Romans giving each other presents during their feast in honour of Saturn and the Norsemen believing that their god Woden brought them gifts at midwinter. The early churchmen could not be seen to condone a pagan custom so they made the winter present-giver . . . St Nicholas!

But after the Protestant reformation of the sixteenth century had led to a lessening of emphasis on saints in England, St Nicholas somehow became merged with the old Father Christmas of the mummers' plays, no saint or archbishop he but a cheery fellow crowned with holly.

Then in the nineteenth century the Americans (who had taken over the tradition from Dutch immigrants 300 years before) polished up their Santa Claus' image in line with the new romantic view of Christmas. They made him into the lovable plump old character we know today, respectably clad in red with white hair and beard; they also substituted reindeer for his horse.

In Britain now presents are given at Christmas and stockings put out (perhaps in memory of the girls whose dowry gold fell into stockings hung up to dry) on Christmas Eve for Father Christmas to fill when he comes down the chimney. (Considerate hosts also leave him a drink, a mince pie and some sprouts for his reindeer!)

In other European countries, however, the twin traditions exist side by side. In Germany, for instance, lucky children have a visit from St Nicholas and, on Christmas Eve, from the Christkindl, a fair-haired girl with a crown of candles who brings a basket of presents to each house. She is a messenger from the Christ child.

Other countries follow the old tradition of present-giving but have different ways of going about it. In Scandinavia Julenisse, a gnome, leaves gifts under the Christmas tree and the children leave porridge out for him. In Russia it is Grandfather Frost who brings the presents.

In Spain and Italy children have to wait until Twelfth Night (6th January). Spanish children leave shoes out for a present and straw for the camels – for it is the Three Kings who bring their presents, just as they did to the baby Jesus, though they are never seen. In Italy La Befana, an old woman who was left behind by the Three Kings on that first trip, comes on her broomstick and climbs down chimneys to leave presents, like Father Christmas. As Christmas approaches children in many countries write in great numbers to Father Christmas in his various guises (such as Père Noël in France) in the hope that the letters sent flying up the chimney or simply posted to the North Pole, Iceland or Greenland will bring the required response in the form of that new bicycle, doll or puppy which will be waiting for them on Christmas morning amidst a host of other exciting presents.

FATHER CHRISTMAS
Painting by K. Roger
*The traditional belief in Santa Claus leaving presents
for children stems from a pagan custom of exchanging
gifts at this time of year*

TRADITIONAL CHRISTMAS FARE

IN EARLIER CENTURIES FOOD SUPPLIES could run very low in winter and people looked forward to enjoying a feast when the animals whose feed (such as the beechnuts and acorns of the pig) was exhausted, were slaughtered. This tied in with their natural desire to have something special to eat on the occasion of an important festival. For many this was indeed a fattened pig, its head (the boar's head of the famous carol) traditionally presented at table crowned with rosemary and with an apple in its mouth. (We still eat sausages and bacon with our turkey today.)

The feast was, as it is today, a central feature of the Christmas festival in most homes, whether eaten on Christmas Eve as in Germany and Austria or on Christmas Day itself. In the households of the great the feasting would have been lavish, typically with a choice of venison, peacock, swan, beef, capon and, after about the time of Henry VIII, turkey. The latter is sometimes known as the Indian peacock and is thought originally to hail from the New World, brought back by Spanish adventurers and introduced to Britain by Turkish merchants, whence the name. Christmas fare at court one year in the reign of Henry V also featured a staggering variety of fish, including salmon, pike, lobster, lampreys, carp and roach.

The less well-off would settle for a joint of pork or a cured ham. In Austria special pork sausages were served at Christmas. Goose has also been a popular choice for Christmas dinner over the centuries; the idea generally has always been to have a treat, something not available every day – for instance fish is often served in countries far from the sea, and this may account for the way we generally tend to eat turkey only at Christmas time.

By the nineteenth century turkey was the usual Christmas meat and this was what Scrooge bought for the Cratchit family on Christmas morning in Dickens' *A Christmas Carol*, although they had already got a goose, which they served with potatoes and apple sauce, the children eating until 'steeped in sage and onions to the eyebrows'. Their goose was followed by a splendid Christmas pudding, such as we would still eat today but vastly different in its composition from the plum porridge it started as centuries before.

Old recipes show that plum porridge was made with meat broth, thickened with breadcrumbs and flavoured with the dried plums (prunes) that gave it its name, raisins, currants, sugar, ginger and other spices, and wines. This was served as a first course until some time in the eighteenth century when it became more solid and was boiled in a cloth. By the early nineteenth century meat was no longer an ingredient at all and a pudding we would recognize today was served as a dessert, flaming with brandy and topped with a seasonal sprig of holly.

Christmas cake, a rich fruit cake, seems not to have much of a history before the reign of Queen Victoria though Mrs Beeton routinely gives a recipe for it in her *Book of Household Management* of 1859. Mince pies, on the other hand, have been associated with Christmas since Tudor times at least: Ben Jonson, the Elizabethan playwright, refers to them in a play and the early

CHRISTMAS PUDDING
This illustration, now housed in the Victoria and Albert Museum, shows a stage in the lengthy preparations of elaborate Christmas fare, such an essential part of the festivities

THE CHRISTMAS HAMPER
Oil painting by Robert Braithwaite Martineau
(1826-69)

seventeenth-century poet Robert Herrick wrote, 'the meat is shredding; For the rare mince-pie' in anticipation of a treat to come.

At this time mince pies were rectangular (and referred to as 'coffins') to represent the manger in which Jesus was born, and were actually made of minced meat as the poem shows, but later dried fruit and spices were first added to, then substituted for the meat. Now only a few ounces of suet in the list of ingredients remind us of the original recipe.

Crib-shaped mince pies were however unfortunately denounced by the Puritans as idolatrous and papist, as was the tiny pastry 'baby' sometimes put on the crust, and the eating of mince pies was forbidden under their all-embracing ban on Christmas celebrations. When they came back into favour with the Restoration of 1660 they were made round as they are today, and no longer bore a 'baby' on top. Superstitions attaching to mince pies have varied from it being considered unlucky to refuse a mince pie at all to lucky to eat one on each of the twelve days of Christmas (in Jamaica today this latter belief extends to the eating of twelve pieces of their very rich Christmas pudding). Christmas sweets, like our mince pies, often include nuts and honey among their ingredients because of old beliefs that nuts promoted fertility in the earth and that honey would serve to sweeten the coming new year.

MRS BEETON'S CHRISTMAS CAKE

INGREDIENTS

5 teacupfuls of flour, 1 teacupful of melted butter, 1 teacupful of cream, 1 teacupful of treacle, 1 teacupful of moist sugar, 2 eggs, ½ oz. of powdered ginger, ½ lb. of raisins, 1 teaspoonful of carbonate of soda, 1 tablespoonful of vinegar.

Mode.—*Make the butter sufficiently warm to melt it, but do not allow it to oil; put the flour into a basin; add to it the sugar, ginger, and raisins, which should be stoned and cut into small pieces. When these dry ingredients are thoroughly mixed, stir in the butter, cream, treacle, and well-whisked eggs, and beat the mixture for a few minutes. Dissolve the soda in the vinegar, add it to the dough, and be particular that these latter ingredients are well incorporated with the others; put the cake into a buttered mould or tin, place it in a moderate oven immediately, and bake it from 1¾ to 2¼ hours.*

Time.—*1¾ to 2¼ hours.*

Average cost, 1s 6d.

TODAY CHRISTMAS EVE IN BRITAIN IS mainly seen as a time for last-minute preparations for Christmas Day but in the past it had its own traditions.

Mummers' plays were usually performed on Christmas Eve, as was the lively ceremony of hauling home the Yule log – in England usually ash, in Scotland birch – which had been previously cut down and left to dry out. Once in position on the hearth the Yule log was lit from a burning piece of last year's log which had been saved specially, sometimes kept under the bed of the lady of the house as a charm against fire, the idea being that it was saving its own fire for Christmas. This custom was also current in Germany and in France where they still make their Christmas cake in the form of a chocolate log.

THE TRADITIONS OF CHRISTMAS EVE

A less widespread custom was the English one of the 'Dumb Cake', which was a sort of loaf baked on Christmas Eve by any single girl wanting to find out who she would marry. She made the cake alone and in silence, pricked it with her initials then went to bed, leaving the door open. At midnight her husband-to-be was supposed to enter and prick his initials next to hers. A variation involved the husband-to-be coming in and just turning the cake as it cooked in the oven.

Midnight on Christmas Eve is of course primarily the time for Midnight Mass and for the tolling of bells announcing the death of the devil and the coming of Christ: the Devil's Knell of Dewsbury in Yorkshire, for instance, tolls once for every year since Christ's birth.

Midnight is also the time when, legend says, animals become able to speak like humans and when bees hum a song in praise of Christ. Evil spirits temporarily lose their powers and, according to an Irish story, the gates of

Paradise open so that anyone who dies at that hour goes straight to heaven.

Back down on earth, Christmas Eve is the time for last-minute jobs to be hastily completed, and for the finishing touches to be made after weeks of hectic preparation. This is the traditional day for decorating the house, and for dressing the Christmas tree. For many households, decorating the tree is a very special family occasion, young and old joining in the fun.

Last, but certainly not least, comes the excitement of hanging up the Christmas stockings and seeing the children creep off to bed in the hope of catching a glimpse of Father Christmas. But somehow, every year, he seems to arrive just when sleepy eyelids have grown heavy and have finally closed!

THE CHRISTMAS VISIT
Illustration by John Charlton, 'The Graphic', 1892

CHRISTMAS MORNING
Painting by Thom. Falcon Marshall (1818-78)

THE DAY AFTER CHRISTMAS DAY, 26th December, has been known in Britain as Boxing Day since the Middle Ages because of the alms boxes which used to be placed in churches at Christmas time to collect money for Christmas food for the poor and opened on that day by the priests.

It is thought that the Romans brought this type of collecting box to Britain although they used them for quite different purposes – to collect money for the games which took place during their winter celebrations.

The custom of the 'dole of the Christmas Box' continued until the Protestant Reformation in the sixteenth century. When it came to an end it seems that the poor began to collect on their own behalf, going round to the houses of the

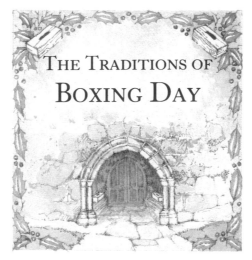

THE TRADITIONS OF BOXING DAY

better-off on the day which had previously been assigned to the sharing out of the Christmas Box, in the hope of reviving the old custom!

It appears also to have been usual for apprentices and household servants to ask for money from their masters and their masters' customers at Christmas and for these gifts to have been kept in an earthenware 'box' with a slit in the top, until they were broken open on 26th December – Boxing Day! (Piggy banks of this sort, that have to be broken to get at the contents, may have got their name, and shape, from the fact that the pig is the only domestic animal that is of no benefit to man until dead, or in this case broken.)

Boxing Day used also to be the day on which those who had provided services through the year, such as lamplighters, dustmen and tradesmen, came to the house for a tip. Nowadays, of course, 'Christmas boxes' are given to postmen, milkmen and so on in the week or so leading up to Christmas Day.

St Stephen's Day

The feast of St Stephen also falls on 26th December. St Stephen was stoned to death for his faith in A.D. 33; he was the first Christian martyr, dying soon after the Crucifixion.

This St Stephen, through connection with another St Stephen of the ninth century, has for long been associated with horses. Over the centuries various traditions have been observed to do with horses on 26th December.

In Germany horsemen would ride around inside the church during the St Stephen's Day service and in Austria and England horses were ceremoniously 'bled' to ensure their good health for the year. The Boxing Day fox hunt in England may well derive from this connection of St Stephen with horses.

ICE SKATING, 1860
Outdoor sports have long been enjoyed on Boxing Day

THE POSTMAN
One of the workers who well deserves his tip

The most characteristically English New Year custom was that of the Watch Night vigil. People still gather together today to eat, drink, dance and play games while waiting for church bells to toll out the old year and to ring in the new. Then we toast the New Year, and sing *Auld Lang Syne* to our friends. In the nineteenth century people would hurry out at midnight with gifts of food and drink for their neighbours.

A Watch Night service, a practice begun about 150 years ago by the Wesleyans, is also held in many churches. Held during the last hour of the old year, this service culminates in a period of silent waiting followed by a hymn of praise and thanksgiving.

Every country, sometimes every county, has its own New Year traditions,

THE TRADITIONS OF NEW YEAR

from settling old debts to drinking and singing in the streets, from bell-ringing competitions to wassailing apple trees. Doors or windows are opened to let the old year out and the new in, and in the Channel Islands a figure of Old Father Time is ceremoniously buried in the sand. In Spain, 12 grapes eaten at midnight, one for each stroke of the clock, bring good luck for the coming year.

Janus, after whom the month of January is named, is the Roman god of doorways and new beginnings. He is usually represented with two heads, one looking back to the past, the other looking forward to the future.

The most potent New Year traditions, however, come today from Scotland where Hogmanay is heartily, often riotously, celebrated, though one of its most important elements, first-footing, was once common in England as well.

The first person to set foot in a house in the New Year will decide its luck for the year. To bring good luck it seems to

be agreed generally that this person should be a male bearing gifts of bread, salt and coal. Each area has its own ideas about the 'lucky' colour of the first-footer's hair but all agree that it should never be a woman.

In many countries New Year's Day is a time for visiting and for giving presents, as it was once in England. In Russia Grandfather Frost brings gifts at New Year. While people now make resolutions about their future behaviour, New Year's Day used to be marked by even more rituals to ensure good luck for the household in the coming year, such as sprinkling everywhere with newly drawn water, or by games to discover one's fate – for instance, by dropping molten lead into cold water and analysing the resulting shape.

Old Father Time and the Young New Year, 1887

Asking for New Year's cakes from house to house on the Isle of Man

The Twelve Days of Christmas end with Twelfth Night, or Epiphany, when the three kings from the East, Caspar, Melchior and Balthasar, arrived with their gifts in Bethlehem to honour and celebrate the birth of the baby Jesus.

Nowadays our attitude to Twelfth Night is rather prosaic, the event being marked mainly by the taking down of the Christmas cards and decorations and the putting out of the Christmas tree. To leave them in position any longer is said to invite bad luck.

More or less isolated instances of old traditions persist. One is the church service held at St James's Palace in London, where members of the Royal Household (once it was the reigning monarch) present the Chapel Royal with gold, frankincense and myrrh in re-

The Traditions of
Twelfth Night

membrance of the first Epiphany. Another is the Baddeley Cake, eaten by the cast of the play currently performing at the Theatre Royal, Drury Lane, as stipulated in the will of Robert Baddeley, an eighteenth-century actor. And in the West of England wassailing ceremonies are carried out on Twelfth Night, cider being sprinkled on the apple trees to ensure their fertility in the coming year.

In many European countries, however, Twelfth Night is still kept as a feast day with family parties and presents for the children. The French continue the custom of the Twelfth Night cake (their *Galette des Rois*) which used to be observed in England. This cake is baked with a bean in it; whoever finds the bean in his or her piece is king or queen for the day and may choose a consort to rule over the party with them.

In Spain children leave out their shoes on Twelfth Night in the hope that the Three Kings will pass by, and fill the waiting shoes with presents.

In the past this feast was notable for its

good luck rituals, its religious processions and its spirit of revelry and good humour. Farmers drank and cheered round bonfires to drive evil spirits from their fields and farms and joined in guessing games, having for instance in one popular game to guess what was cooking on the kitchen spit (and this might be something silly, such as an old shoe!) before being allowed back in the house.

In the street the fools and hobby-horses of the Morris men joined the apprentices in playing practical jokes and these were also popular at court. Feasting and the playing of games, especially games of chance, were universal, and in general everyone made the most of the last of the Christmas holiday – much as we do in the twentieth century.

Family parties were, and still are, popular on Twelfth Night

Plays and pantomimes are frequently enjoyed as a lively end to the festive season

Christmas CHRONICLE

On the twelfth day of Christmas my true love sent to me
Twelve ladies dancing,
Eleven lords a-leaping,
Ten drummers drumming,
Nine pipers piping,
Eight maids a-milking,
Seven swans a-swimming,
Six geese a-laying,
Five gold rings,
Four calling birds,
Three French hens,
Two turtle doves,
And a partridge in a pear tree.

From *The Twelve Days of Christmas*, anon.

ADVENT IS A TIME OF ANTICIPATION and of preparations, not only in a religious sense but in practical terms. Organize yourself properly this Christmas so that the work you have to do to make it a success – and there is no doubt that work is necessary – will serve to heighten this sense of excitement and anticipation rather than merely bring on unseasonal exhaustion and bad temper.

Avoid last-minute panic by buying and making as much in advance as possible, within reason – it does seem to spoil the effect if presents are seen to be bought in September and cards written in October!

In the realm of food, of course, it is often necessary to work well in advance, as many traditional Christmas foods improve with keeping. Indeed by tradition Christmas puddings and cakes had to be made by the Sunday before Advent if they were to be ready for Christmas. This was popularly known as Stir or Stir Up Sunday because of the collect for the church service that day: 'Stir up we beseech thee, O Lord, the wills of thy faithful people ...' Nothing to do with making a wish as you stir the pudding mixture!

Home-made mincemeat also improves as it matures and the flavours blend. Some versions need to be kept in the refrigerator, using valuable space, but others will do quite well in a cool cupboard: if the mincemeat dries out at all, drip in a little brandy before using.

When you are planning your Christmas cooking, take into account any gifts of food you might want to make. Give a Christmas cake or pudding, tied up in ribbon and presented in its own tin or

THINKING WELL AHEAD

bowl. People without cooking facilities (or abilities) and those who are overloaded with Christmas cooking will both appreciate this sort of thoughtfulness. Jars of mincemeat or chutney for the post-Christmas cold meats also make good presents.

Present-giving is another sphere where advance thought is valuable even if no actual buying is done early. Keep

Now thrice welcome, Christmas,
which brings us good cheer,
Mince pies and plum porridge,
good ale and strong beer;
With pig, goose and capon,
the best that may be,
So well doth the weather
and our stomachs agree.

Poor Robin's Almanack (1695)

your ears and eyes open for hints from your family as to what they want or need and jot down any good ideas, making a note of the details or the address of the supplier. And don't just trail around the usual shops in your quest for gifts: investigate the many excellent postal offers which are advertised widely in newspapers and magazines.

Order magazine subscriptions for presents through the post, whether you choose a specialist publication to suit the known interests of the recipient or something with a wider appeal that they might not otherwise buy. (Or buy a season ticket to a local zoo or football stadium.)

Houseplants, miniature roses and cut flowers can all be sent as presents by ordering through the post. Early daffodils make a particularly lovely surprise – and a refreshing antidote to an overdose of red and green!

In connection with the postal services, here is an idea for a present for children who find it hard to get down to thank-you letters: several firms make up sets of special 'thank-you' notelets decorated with popular characters such as Peter Rabbit or Raymond Briggs' Snowman and printed with 'Thank you' at the top so the child has only to continue his or her letter. These make it a positive pleasure to write the thank-you letters whose absence is so often bemoaned by generous grandparents.

Postal presents are of course ideal for those who simply cannot get out to the shops. Many worthwhile charities publish mail-order catalogues with gifts in a wide price range, giving you the chance to contribute to a good cause.

GOOD FOOD PLAYS A CENTRAL ROLE in the Christmas festivities, with the main Christmas dinner as the high point. The fact that tradition plays a large part in deciding the menu both helps to simplify planning for the cook and lays a burden on him or her to outdo the dinners of every previous year.

Most people today plump for turkey although roast goose, rib of beef or a joint of pork are all popular. Vary your family's 'turkey experience' by trying out new stuffings: celery and apricot, chestnut, sausagemeat, apple and lemon, as well as sage and onion. Or try oyster stuffing, still made in the United States though more or less forgotten in Britain. Cook one sort in the cavity of the turkey and one separately.

Give the traditional accompaniments a new touch: add almonds or walnuts and crisp breadcrumbs to the sprouts and make the bacon and chipolatas into mini-kebabs with cocktail sticks. Or break away from the usual vegetables to include red cabbage cooked with apple, or creamed carrots or celeriac.

When it's time for Christmas pudding, however strong the tradition – and no-one would wish to cut out the thrill of the entrance of the pudding, flaming in brandy – so many of us find we just cannot face anything heavy and children tend not to be great fans anyway. So prepare a light, fresh alternative, a fruit sorbet, chilled orange soufflé or a simple mixture of fresh fruits such as melon and lychees.

The other meals we eat at Christmas time do require more thought if we are not to bore everyone with variations on turkey, or overload them with too much

SEASONAL MEALS AND MENUS

rich food. Cast your net wide: recipes for spiced beef, marinated in sugar, salt and spices then baked very slowly, go back at least three hundred years and its mellow, spicy flavour will be ideal for a Boxing Day cold spread. Smoked collar of bacon (which can be cooked the week before and kept foil-wrapped in the fridge) is also delicious – and no trouble!

Serve with tangy fresh salads: the classic winter salad of celery, apple and beetroot; potatoes and button mushrooms in a creamy blend of yogurt, mayonnaise and French mustard, garnished with parsley, or watercress and orange salad with walnuts.

In your quest for dishes to counterpoint the turkey, look also at the wide range of recipes more recently introduced to Britain from India: haddock baked in a yogurt sauce or cod steaks in a spicy tomato sauce make easily prepared meals for Christmas Eve for instance, and don't forget the Indian relishes and pickles when you are eating cold meats – brinjal (aubergine) pickle will come as a very pleasant surprise to your taste buds after the blandness of turkey.

Your best friend, if you want a relaxed Christmas with good home-made food, is your refrigerator or freezer. Many of the foods described above can be prepared before the holiday and frozen until you need them, as also can bread sauce, brandy or rum butter, mince pies, and treats – to deploy as needed – such as pâtés, fish mousses and prawns (to be served with a dip of yogurt, mayonnaise and French mustard and eaten on Christmas morning with a glass of champagne or sparkling white wine).

With a well-stocked refrigerator or freezer you can welcome unexpected guests with generous hospitality without worrying about running out of food. You can have useful raw materials and basic foodstuffs to hand as well as made-up dishes: bread for instance freezes well as does the dough for cheese biscuits to have with drinks.

Finally, use the refrigerator to ensure a plentiful supply of chilled wine and the freezer for ice cubes for spirits. Put loose ice cubes, once made, in plastic bags and pop them in the freezer until you need them. Drinkers of mineral waters also often prefer their tipple cold so keep a bottle ready chilled.

SUPERLATIVE
MINCEMEAT

Take four large lemons with their weight of golden pippins pared and cored, of jar-raisins, candied citron and orange-rind; and the finest suet, and a fourth part more of sugar.

Boil the lemons tender, chop them small, but be careful just to extract the pips. Add them to the other ingredients after all have been prepared with great nicety, and mix the whole well with from three to four glasses of good brandy, a pinch of salt, some nutmeg and mace and ginger (two whole nutmegs going to 10lb mincemeat plus one large teaspoon of pounded mace and rather more of ginger).

From Modern Cookery for Private Families
by Eliza Acton,
1845

CHRISTMAS CARDS

Greetings cards have become an essential part of our Christmas, keeping us in touch with a network of family and friends in the long term as well as simply extending seasonal good wishes. For this reason we value the cards we receive and feel pleased when others remember us.

Don't hurt the feelings of those to whom you usually send cards by forgetting anyone or by sending cards late. Make a Christmas card list and keep it up to date. Note down 'last posting' dates for all the various categories, home and overseas, as soon as they are announced by the Post Office, and buy as many Christmas stamps as you will need as soon as they come out – the queues later on can be pretty daunting. Don't forget the Post Office's special offer books of stamps, when they are available.

Buy your Christmas cards early too, before the range of choice narrows; the same goes for wrapping-paper, ribbon and gift tags.

When sending a card to someone they don't see very often many people like to enclose a long 'newsy' letter. Don't leave this until the last minute or you may be tempted not to bother, and regret it later. Set aside a quiet evening early in December to do this, to write your cards and to wrap any presents that have to be posted off early. Indeed, there is a lot to be said for wrapping as many presents as possible well in advance: secret rustlings of wrapping-paper on Christmas Eve do give a thrill of excitement but wrapping gifts early gives you a chance to do something a bit special (see page 68) – and there are other things to do on

CHRISTMAS EVE
Detail of oil painting by George Bernard O'Neill

ARRANGING A TROUBLE-FREE CHRISTMAS

Christmas Eve after all, like relaxing and enjoying it in tranquillity.

If you have your Christmas cards printed with your own personal greetings, be sure to make your order in good time so you can enjoy choosing the wording and typeface you want rather than rushing in and picking just anything at the last minute.

TRAVEL

If you have to travel over the holiday period take steps to ensure that all your journeys will be trouble-free. If you are going under your own steam, have your car serviced in good time and always check on road conditions before you set out for a long trip or if the weather is at all tricky. Don't be let down by your own condition either: don't drink and drive. If you are going out to dinner or to a party, book a taxi to take you and to collect you at a prearranged time so you don't have to think about staying below the limit – or falling out with your partner over who stays off the alcohol!

If you travel by public transport, remember that there will be great numbers of other people following more or less the same time scheme as you as far as coming and going is concerned. Make reservations well in advance for journeys by air and for coach trips. If you go by train, get your ticket beforehand to avoid queues and treat yourself to a reserved seat: when you arrive at the crowded railway station the wonderful sense of security that comes from knowing you will be able to sit down is well worth the slight expense and bother of making the arrangement as well as ensuring that you arrive refreshed.

HOSPITALITY

Christmas has always been a time for being hospitable, especially in the large households of the past. If you are in a position to offer hospitality, either for the day or for someone to stay over the holiday, be sure not to leave it too late before you do so. Those friends, members of the family, or indeed strangers contacted through social services departments, who might otherwise spend Christmas alone, and lonely, will feel really wanted if they are asked early and will enjoy the anticipation as well as having a chance to make any arrangements necessary.

Potential party guests also appreciate advance warning so they can fit in to what is often a busy schedule over Christmas. At a time when there are many social events on, you will not want to risk a thin array of guests or miss out on someone else's party because it clashes with your own.

Be merry all,
Be merry all,
With holly dress the festive hall;
Prepare the song,
The feast, the ball,
To welcome merry
Christmas.

W. R. Spencer

Christmas cover,
'Illustrated London News', 1895.
By this time the sending of cards had become a
Christmas ritual

CHESTNUT SAUCE AND STUFFING

Roast and skin 1½lb of chestnuts for the stuffing and allow about as many for the sauce. Stuff the turkey's crop with chicken forcemeat. Fill the body with the peeled, roasted chestnuts, salt, pepper and about 8 oz butter. Roast the turkey as usual.

For the sauce simmer some roasted peeled chestnuts in ½ pint of good stock. When they are tender thicken the stock with a nut of butter rolled in flour, stirring it in till smooth and free of lumps. Add diced fried gammon and small fried sausages, cut in slices, just before it is served.

From The Art of Cookery
Made Plain and Easy
by Hannah Glasse,
1747

OLD-FASHIONED VICTUALS

A VICTORIAN FEAST

Heaped up on the floor, to form a kind of throne, were turkeys, geese, game, poultry, brawn, great joints of meat, sucking pigs, long wreaths of sausages, mince-pies, plum-puddings, barrels of oysters, red-hot chestnuts, cherry-cheeked apples, juicy oranges, luscious pears, immense twelfth cakes, and seeth-ing bowls of punch, that made the chamber dim with their delicious steam....

From A Christmas Carol
by Charles Dickens,
1843

PLUM PUDDING

Two pounds and a quarter of stoned raisins, two pounds and a quarter of currants, six ounces of finely-chopped candied peel, thirteen eggs, one pint and a half of milk, one teacupful and a half of bread-crumbs, one pound and a half of flour, one pound and a half of finely chopped suet, three wineglasses of brandy, two wineglasses of rum.

Mix these ingredients well together, put into buttered basins, and boil for fourteen hours. This quantity makes two large puddings.

From The Ocklye Cookery Book
by Eleanor L. Jenkinson,
1909

— December 1st —

If you have not already made an Advent calendar, buy one and let the children open the first window.

— 2nd —

Order your turkey, goose or any large joints of meat for Christmas and New Year to make sure you get just what you want — not what is left over. Plan your menu for the whole period of the holiday.

— 3rd —

Buy Christmas cards, tape, wrapping-paper and get your calendar and diary for next year. Book up for a pantomime.

— 4th —

Cook and freeze mince pies, sausage rolls, biscuit dough and a selection of quiches and made-up dishes of the piquant variety so you need not worry about cooking over the Christmas period.

— 5th —

Set aside a day for present shopping after making a detailed list of what you want to get. Note down any clothes sizes necessary. Write any long letters you want to include with your Christmas cards.

— 6th —

Invite people if you are entertaining at Christmas — if you have not done so before. Let them know if you'll be providing food.

DAY-BY-DAY PLANNING

— 7th —

Take out your Christmas cake and cover with marzipan. Write the bulk of your Christmas cards.

— 8th —

If you have decided to have an open fire in the sitting-room for an old-fashioned atmosphere for Christmas, get in the coal and/or logs. Give logs a chance to dry out to avoid a smoky room.

— 9th —

Have another day for present shopping. Wrap as many presents as you can at this stage.

— 10th —

Do a giant shop for non-perishable goods — everything you or your guests might need from tins of smoked oysters to have with drinks to a good supply of toilet paper!

— 11th —

Make sure you have a supply of coins or notes of the right denomination to give as tips to the dustmen, milkmen, and so on. This avoids embarrassment if you have too little and resentment if you feel you have been forced into giving more than you really wanted to.

— 12th —

Give the milkman your order for milk, cream, yogurt and so on for the Christmas period when he will probably be very busy and working to a tight schedule.

— 13th —

Get in your supply of Christmas drinks, including anything unusual you may need for cocktails, champagne or sparkling wine for Christmas morning and New Year's Eve and claret for Christmas dinner. Don't forget to provide fruit juice or mineral water for children and for those avoiding alcohol.

— 14th —

Look out for a carol concert to attend; many churches and local choirs present these, sometimes in aid of charity.

— 15th —

Visit the hairdresser so you feel you are looking your best for the festivities. If you opt for a new style, you'll have got to grips with it by the time Christmas comes round.

— 16th —

Get out your Christmas cake and ice and decorate it.

— 17th —

Buy the Christmas tree and stand it in water, preferably in the garden or somewhere cool, until you are ready to decorate it. Get the children to sit down and write to Father Christmas and send the letters off to 'Father Christmas, c/o North Pole'.

— 18th —

Make new Christmas decorations and check the old ones, particularly the lights for the tree which seem always to be temperamental.

— 19th —

Go carol-singing in aid of your favourite charity. Take song sheets to avoid faltering voices.

— 20th —

Gather holly and ivy or buy if you live in town. Collect pine cones and tree ivy to spray silver. Make popcorn if you are going to use it to decorate your tree – and make biscuits for the tree.

— 21st —

Do last-minute present shopping and wrap everything. Put up the decorations and a welcoming wreath on the front door. Decorate the tree. This will cheer up your 'shortest day' quite considerably.

— 22nd —

Do last-minute food shopping: oranges, nuts, cheeses and so on. Make brandy or rum butter and store it in the fridge.

— 23rd —

Make stuffing and put in fridge. Collect turkey and other meat. If you have a large frozen bird then start to defrost it.

— 24th —

Don't save all the treats until tomorrow; let the festivities begin! In the evening take ready-made food from freezer, hang up your stockings and put out food for Santa and his reindeer, and if you are really organized do the vegetables and lay the table for tomorrow.

— 25th —

Christmas Day. Enjoy yourself! Preparing Christmas dinner may dominate the day but don't let it take over completely. Make a note of who gave what to whom.

— 26th —

With the pressure, however pleasant, off, go to a pantomime, football match or race meeting.

— 27th —

Back to work for most people. If you are still at home, try to see those friends or relatives you couldn't manage to see on Christmas Day or Boxing Day.

— 28th —

The children will be off school for a while. Give them some attention so they get the best out of their new toys, especially those that require adult assistance or supervision.

— 29th —

Get down to the thank-you letters promptly; it makes the job easier and more pleasant. Use the list you compiled on Christmas Day – you'll find it indispensable.

— 30th —

Transfer all your details, addresses and the like, to your new diary.

— 31st —

Give or go to a New Year's Eve party – or at least stay up to toast the New Year in. Play fortune-telling games such as throwing the lead to get the party spirit.

— January 1st —

Take stock of your life and make your New Year Resolutions.

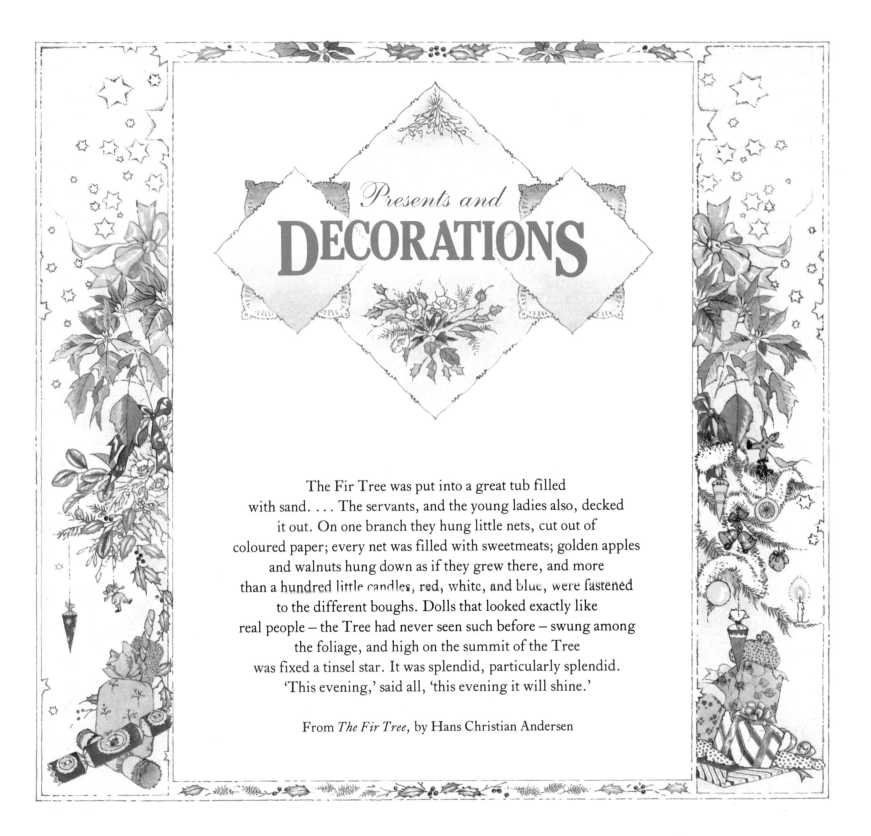

Presents and DECORATIONS

The Fir Tree was put into a great tub filled
with sand. . . . The servants, and the young ladies also, decked
it out. On one branch they hung little nets, cut out of
coloured paper; every net was filled with sweetmeats; golden apples
and walnuts hung down as if they grew there, and more
than a hundred little candles, red, white, and blue, were fastened
to the different boughs. Dolls that looked exactly like
real people – the Tree had never seen such before – swung among
the foliage, and high on the summit of the Tree
was fixed a tinsel star. It was splendid, particularly splendid.
'This evening,' said all, 'this evening it will shine.'

From *The Fir Tree*, by Hans Christian Andersen

MAKE A CHRISTMAS CRIB

Central to our celebration of Christmas is the Nativity. In many countries the crib is an important feature of the Christmas decorations.

To make your own crib scene, use stiff paper to make the bodies of your people. Draw round a plate on the paper (*fig* 1), cut out and use half of each circle to form a cone, glued or sellotaped at the back (*fig* 2). Make beards and arms with stiff paper (*fig* 3); slot them through the cone or stick them round the front.

Make the heads with small paper or polystyrene balls: cut a round in the top of the cone, drop the ball in place and secure from underneath with plasticine. Or use a table tennis ball: cut a hole in it and glue it on to the point of the cone.

Paint the faces on the balls with poster paint and add features with felt-tip pens or by sticking on tiny scraps of sticky-backed paper. For hair or beards, glue on wool, cotton wool or unwoven string.

To 'dress' the figures, either paint the cones and add a cloak, or make a full robe to cover the whole cone. Paint the arms to match in either case. Give Joseph and the shepherds headdresses tied round with cord, and the kings crowns of foil or a fabric turban.

Make the baby Jesus from plasticine with a bead head stuck on. Use a felt-tip pen to mark on eyes, nose and mouth and wrap in a strip of white paper tissue, leaving only the face uncovered. Glue a tiny circle of yellow or gold paper to the back of Jesus's head to make a halo.

For the manger, use the inner part of a matchbox with cardboard legs held on by split pins. Put hay under Jesus.

To make the stable, cut away the sides of a cardboard box, leaving corner supports. Paint as you wish. Cover the floor with straw or hay.

You can also make your own animals with different coloured plasticine.

fig 1

fig 2

fig 3

Make an Advent Calendar

ADVENT, FROM THE LATIN 'TO come', refers to the coming of Jesus Christ and covers the four weeks leading up to Christmas. It is a time of preparation. On Advent calendars, each day from December 1st, a little numbered window may be opened until on Christmas Eve the last one reveals the Nativity scene.

Tree Calendar

To make a pyramid shaped tree, you will need a piece of thin green card 105 x 26.5 cm (36 x 10⅜in) and three sheets of white drawing paper 35 x 26.5 cm (12 x 10⅜in). Make the white sheets into equilateral triangles, each side measuring 35 cm (12 in). Use them as templates to form the green card into a boat shape. Place two of them against the top edge of the card, points downwards and fit the third in between, point up. Rule a line around this shape. Put the white sheets aside, and cut out the green card. Cut a long narrow flap from the left-over green card and fix it to one slanting edge with adhesive tape.

Fold the card into pyramid form so that the fold lines are clear and open it out flat. On each side, mark 8 'windows' in shapes like presents and number them 1 to 24. Cut out all but one side of each window with a craft knife, and fold them open. To draw the scenes behind the windows, lay a white triangle behind each side of the green card in turn and mark exactly where each picture should fall. Colour in a tiny illustration to fit each frame: a candle, robin, star and so

on. Glue the sheets carefully to the back of the card (the inside of the pyramid). Decorate the presents on the tree with printed paper or foil and snippets of ribbon and write the numbers with gold or silver marker pens. Close the windows and re-form the pyramid by glueing down the flap.

Fabric Advent Stocking

Cut the outline of a stocking from a piece of fabric and hem it, or use felt. Sew 24 evenly spaced gold curtain rings on the stocking with two more at the top to hang it up. Make the numbers in each ring with glued-on gold cord, adhesive-backed printed numbers, or in embroidery stitches. To each ring attach a tiny gift (see above) for children to take on each day of Advent. Edible gifts could include brightly wrapped sweets or nuts; small items such as pencil sharpeners or toy animals would also be suitable.

If the children join in making the calendar or stocking do not let them use sharp blades and supervise anyone using needle and thread. Remember that metallic markers are toxic.

If you are tired of sending out shop-bought Christmas cards, attractive as many of them are, only to get the same ones back from other people, have a go at something more distinctive and much more personal. Design and make your own cards; it is easier than you probably think, especially if you don't overstretch yourself and if you follow a few simple ground rules.

Basic Guidelines

Begin by buying a set or sets of envelopes and make your cards 6mm (¼ inch) smaller all round so you know you have envelopes that will fit.

Buy good quality art paper and don't let it get crumpled or grubby. You are looking for a pristine effect.

Use really sharp scissors, a scalpel or a craft knife to cut the paper so that edges are not rough and clumsy looking. Embroidery scissors are good for cutting out intricate shapes.

Don't try anything too ambitious; a simple card is often the most effective.

Making your own Christmas Cards

Victorian Lace Montage

Copy the early Victorian style of Christmas card with a lace-bordered picture. Fold art paper to make the card you want, whether folded at the top or at the side, using, for a slightly nostalgic effect, a pastel or muted colour rather than the bright ones usually associated with Christmas.

Cut a picture from an old Christmas

card or calendar. Choose an old fashioned, even sentimental, picture rather than something comic or modern.

Glue the picture to the front of the card, arranging it centrally with enough space for a greeting if you plan to include one, and for a ribbon trim at the side or top. Cut a length of narrow lace trimming in cream or white one-and-a-half times to twice the diameter of the picture. Sew a line of gathering stitches down the centre of the lace and draw it up to the correct length. Join the edges to make a continuous border frill and glue it around the picture to frame it. If one edge of the trimming is plain or unfinished, it may look better to glue the frame in place first, with the picture on top to hide the raw edge.

Make an inner card for your message from lightweight paper: airmail paper in light brown has a convincingly Victorian look and feel about it. Cut it to about 1.5cm (½ in) smaller all round than the card, fold it in half and slip it in. Use a hole-punch to make two neat holes on the folded edge and thread very narrow satin ribbon through all thicknesses, tying it in a bow at the front. Choose the colour of the ribbon and the lettering of any message to tone with the picture.

Hand-lettered Carol

If you are competent at lettering by hand using pen and ink, write out a verse or verses from a Christmas poem or carol to decorate the front of your card. Choose paper and ink in toning colours for the best effect (good quality paper is particularly important) and finish by drawing a neat border round your work. Do the greeting inside the card in the same way.

Not only is christmas an important milestone in the course of the year, but also in the train of our lives. Keep Christmas memories bright by creating a special album. First choose a book. It must be sturdy, with strong board covers and high grade paper. The easiest choice is a modern photograph album with acetate sheeting to hold the pictures in place. Covering an undistinguished-looking hard-cover book with fabric is not too difficult. Choose a lightweight but hardwearing fabric. Alternatively, all kinds of scrap-books are available. Heavy paper is best, and spiral binding allows you to include bulkier items. You may wish to invest in a leatherbound book, or a beautifully crafted specimen with marbled covers.

Set out the pages with care. Try

Making a Christmas Album

drawing coloured borders round each entry; decorate the corners with a draw-ing or a small motif; number the pages and the items you include.

To cover the album, you will need a piece of fabric large enough to wrap round the book with a 5cm (2in) turn-over all round. Apply a PVA-type glue to the front cover of the book. Lay the closed book down on the wrong side of the fabric. Turn the book and fabric over and smooth the fabric into place, over the cover and into the ridge where the spine meets the cover.

Fold the fabric back, apply glue to the spine, and smooth the fabric over, working it into the ridge beween the spine and the back cover. Finally apply glue to the back cover and smooth the fabric into place. To neaten the spine, make four slits in the fabric, two at the top and two at the bottom, and trim them to 1.5cm (½in). Apply a little glue to the wrong side of each flap and ease them into the hollows of the spine (*fig 1*) with the end of a pencil. Before folding in the fabric on the covers, trim it diagonally at the 4 corners to within 5mm (¼in) of the corners for neatness. Apply glue to the turnovers and smooth down (*fig 2*). To finish off, paste the first page to the inside front cover and the last page to the inside back cover. Leave the book evenly weighted down on a clean flat surface for at least 24 hours or until the glue is completely dry.

fig 1

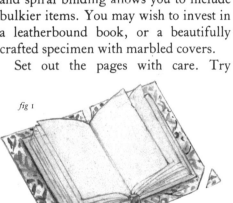

fig 2

Children of all ages can share in the pleasure of preparing for Christmas by making their own Christmas cards. Younger children will require some supervision with scissors and glue and older ones some help with tricky subjects but at any level a child's own work has a special appeal.

The materials are neither expensive nor hard to come by. Art paper and felt-tip pens are available in a wide variety of striking colours. If you prefer to use fine white paper such as typing paper, fold it in half horizontally then again vertically to make a double sheet card which will be firm enough to stand up. Gold or silver metallic pens give an exciting effect to even the simplest design, but they are toxic and children should only use them under supervision. Poster paints are easy to work with – and will wash out of clothes afterwards! Use water colours where you want a more subtle effect. Use any clear-drying paper glue: solid glue sticks are excellent for young children. Double-sided sellotape gives a really neat finish.

Here are some suggestions for cards for children to make, all of which can be adapted to taste and according to the materials available and the artist's skill.

COLLAGE IDEAS

Glue fronds of fern or dried bracken on to card so that each frond makes one branch of a tiny Christmas tree.

Cut snowflakes out of lacy paper doilies (remember snowflakes always have six points or sides) and stick them on to black or another dark coloured paper. Dark blue looks good. Write the greeting with a silver pen.

CHRISTMAS CARDS FOR CHILDREN TO MAKE

Cut out strips of Christmas wrapping-paper and put double-sided sellotape on the back. Cut the strips into candle shapes and arrange them on cheerfully coloured stiff cards. To make the 'flames' use gold gift-wrapping ribbon. Stick double-sided sellotape on the ribbon, cut out simple flame shapes and tuck them into the tops of the candles before sticking them down.

Very small children could cut up old cards and stick them on to clean card.

CUT-OUT SNOWMAN

Draw a plump snowman on a single thickness of stiff white card. Cut him out carefully and colour in his face, hat, scarf and buttons in red and black. Write your Christmas greetings, also in red or black, on the back of the snowman. A hat and scarf cut out of felt and stuck on with glue adds an interesting change of texture. To make the snowman stand up, cut a strip of card about 4cm (1½ in) wide. Fold it over inwards at the top and attach it to the snowman's back at shoulder level. A figure 15cm (6in) high will be supported by a strip of card the same length.

GLUE AND GLITTER

On stiff coloured paper using a felt-tip or metallic pen draw the outline of a fairly simple Christmas symbol such as a bell, a candle or a star (make two overlapping triangles). Spread glue within this outline and sprinkle with gold or silver glitter. Shake off any excess on to a clean sheet of paper so that it can be used again. Write your greeting with the same pen for a unified effect.

POP-OUT CHRISTMAS TREE

Fold a strip of fairly lightweight green paper so that it falls into concertina folds. Paint or stick decorations on to the folded paper: use tiny rounds of foil or coloured cellophane, such as sweet wrappers, and single threads of tinsel. Stick it inside a card so that the outer folds run nearly to a point at the top. Close the card and press firmly. Cut the lower edge of the tree zigzag fashion.

On the card itself, draw or paint a trunk and pot for the tree and top it with a star. Write your Christmas message on the front of the card, enclosed in a border, and put who it is from on the inside.

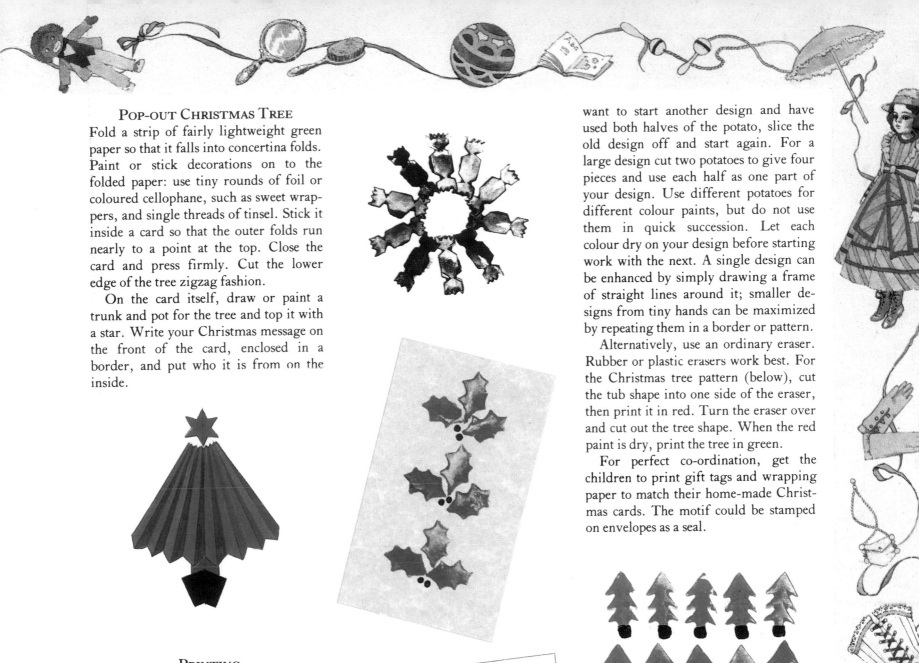

PRINTING

Print a pattern or picture with corks, pine cones, pieces of sponge and so on — in fact anything that will transfer colour from the paint to the card (don't use ordinary paper — it is too thin and will crinkle when wet). You can also cut a design into a potato — a simple cross or a star perhaps — and use this. When you want to start another design and have used both halves of the potato, slice the old design off and start again. For a large design cut two potatoes to give four pieces and use each half as one part of your design. Use different potatoes for different colour paints, but do not use them in quick succession. Let each colour dry on your design before starting work with the next. A single design can be enhanced by simply drawing a frame of straight lines around it; smaller designs from tiny hands can be maximized by repeating them in a border or pattern.

Alternatively, use an ordinary eraser. Rubber or plastic erasers work best. For the Christmas tree pattern (below), cut the tub shape into one side of the eraser, then print it in red. Turn the eraser over and cut out the tree shape. When the red paint is dry, print the tree in green.

For perfect co-ordination, get the children to print gift tags and wrapping paper to match their home-made Christmas cards. The motif could be stamped on envelopes as a seal.

ONE OF THE JOYS OF CHRISTMAS morning is to find a stocking bulging with goodies and unwrapping them one by one. This stocking may hang on a mantlepiece, at the end of a bed or even on the doorknob to a child's bedroom. There is a special pleasure in making your own stockings, designing a special one for every member of the family.

RED FELT STOCKING

One simple method is to cut two pieces of red felt into a standard stocking shape, perhaps in sizes reflecting the range of ages in the family. Oversew the edges in small stitches, securing firmly, and turn inside out. Glue a border of cotton wool

A jolly red felt stocking, ready to be filled with presents

CHRISTMAS STOCKINGS TO MAKE

all round the top. Holding the sides together, make six holes through all layers and 'lace' through with thick yarn in the colour of your choice. Pompoms at the ends of the bootlace are a colourful and effective finish. Don't forget to stitch a loop at the back so the stocking can be hung up easily.

NEEDLEPOINT STOCKING

In the United States, a marriage of canvaswork embroidery and Christmas tradition has produced a beautiful stocking that can be personalized and will become a cherished family heirloom.

These stockings are 50cm (20 in) in length. They are worked in two strands of Persian yarn on a canvas (mono-canvas) that is 13 holes to the inch. The basic stitch used is basketweave because there is much less distortion to the canvas; tent stitch is suitable, but there may be distortion. As you can see, different yarns and stitches are used to add texture. Santa's beard, for instance, is made in French knots; hair is done

with lots of loops, then cut off and fluffed out.

If you would like to try your hand at this craft, transfer the design grid below, scaled up, square by square, to a paper grid where each square is five times larger than the sample grid. When you are satisfied with the design go over the outlines with a waterproof marking pen and place this under your canvas. Carefully trace the design on to the canvas.

Do remember to personalize the design. Insert your child's name or initials and use an appropriate colour yarn for the hair. Perhaps you would want to substitute a dog for the cat in the foreground.

OME-MADE GIFTS HAVE AN IMPACT
out of all proportion to how much
they cost to make or how elaborate they
are. Their appeal comes from the fact
that they are intensely personal, im-
plying real thoughtfulness; your time has
been spent on them and time is a precious
commodity. You do not need a lot of
specialized know-how to make the items
described here; relax, and rely on common sense and your imagination.

EDIBLE GIFTS

Use cotton or lawn in a small print, cut
with pinking shears, to make pretty
covers for pots of home-made mincemeat
or chutney, useful additions to any larder
at this season. Cut circles of fabric 4-5cm
(1½ – 2 in) wider all round than the top
of the jar. For a snug fit, a row of
shirring elastic in the fabric is best.
Alternatively, make a ring of ordinary
elastic to fit and tie a pretty ribbon
around the pot to finish. Try to look out
for unusual or attractive jars throughout

PRETTY
PRESENTS
TO MAKE

the year to use when making jams and
preserves as presents. For a neat finish
buy or make for yourself nicely lettered
labels. Such attention to detail takes very
little time and makes a good deal of
difference to the finished look.

Make up a hamper of goodies by
padding a wooden fruit box with coloured tissue paper and nesting a selection
of jars, suitably trimmed, in this. Cover
the outside of the box with Christmas
wrapping-paper and tie a big floppy bow
on one corner. Pretty – and practical!

MIRROR COVER

Use ready-quilted fabric to make an
attractive protective cover for an ordinary handbag mirror.

Cut the fabric to twice the size of the
mirror plus about 6mm (¼ in) all round
(to allow for seams and so that the mirror
will just slip in and out). Fold fabric in
half and stitch two sides; leave one short
side open. Oversew or zigzag the seams
to stop fraying and bind the opening
with a strip of the same fabric or with

matching or contrasting bias binding.
Turn the cover right side out.

LINED BASKET

Line a tiny basket with fabric to hold a
round tablet of soap or a larger one to use
on the dressing-table or for sewing
accessories. Cut cardboard to fit the base
of the basket and cover with a circle of
fabric slightly larger: make a row of
gathering stitches near the perimeter of
the circle, draw it up and fasten so the
cardboard is enclosed. You could equally
well fix the fabric with glue, snipping
the edges of the circle for ease of fit.

Cut a strip of fabric as deep as the
basket plus 7cm (3 in), and half as long
again as its circumference. Join the short
edges with a flat seam. Stitch a 1.5cm
(½ in) hem on the top edge and gather
it. Draw up evenly and stitch to the top
rim of the basket; clothes pegs will hold
the fabric in place as you work. Apply
adhesive to the wrong side of the fabric-
covered card and stick it in the base of
the basket to conceal the unhemmed
edge. Trim the top edge with lace.

POMANDERS

Make these sweet scented balls by sticking cloves into a whole orange and then
rolling it in a mixture of cinnamon,
nutmeg, all-spice and orris-root. Tie
round with a satin ribbon long enough
for hanging in wardrobes and so on.

MAKING CANDLES

Hand-made candles are a Christmas gift
that is wholly appropriate to the season
and thoroughly individual. Let your
creative imagination have full play with
different colours, shapes and sizes.

All you need is candle wax, which comes in granules, a hardener called stearin and lengths of wick, all of which can be bought at craft suppliers. No special moulds are necessary; use a clean empty yogurt or cream pot or anything similar.

Tie a length of wick to a pencil and lay the pencil across the mould so the wick falls to the centre bottom of the mould; fix it in place with a blob of melted wax. Melt 9 parts wax to 1 part stearin in an old pan; pour in gently. Leave to cool.

For striped candles leave one layer to harden before pouring on another, unless you want to swirl the colours round to get a marbled effect. Glue a piece of felt to the bottom of the candle if you are giving it without a holder.

Candles made and given in sundae or wine glasses make pretty presents but don't pour the wax in until it has cooled a little or it will crack the glass.

LAVENDER BAGS

An old favourite but always welcome to perfume drawers or to tie on coat hangers, lavender bags are easy to make. Cut a piece of fabric about 25cm (10 in) by 10cm (4 in), fold in half lengthways and stitch up two sides to make a bag; turn inside out. If you cut out the fabric with pinking shears, the top and seams will be ready neatened, but a lace trimming would be appropriate.

Fill the bag with dried lavender and tie at the neck with narrow satin ribbon to match the fabric. Add a second, longer ribbon to attach the bag to clothes hangers. Use a fabric with a small print if possible; floral print cotton or Liberty-type lawns are ideal for this purpose.

As with so many of our most delightful Christmas traditions, it was the Victorians who first introduced the Christmas cracker. The invention is credited to an imaginative and commercially minded baker and confectioner from London, named Tom Smith. During a visit to Paris in 1840 he was struck by the pretty wrapping of the French *bonbons*, with coloured papers twisted at either end. On returning to his London shop he promptly applied the idea to his own products, adding a love message and later a snap and a paper hat.

The paper-wrapped sweets, of course, are still obtainable from sweet shops, but the larger version, with frills, paper flowers and scrap pictures, proved particularly popular with the Victorians. Their flair for elaborate, home-made gifts found another outlet in crackers and they used them to commemorate all sorts of special occasions. Nowadays, the Christmas cracker is virtually the sole survivor of this enchanting custom, but once you have mastered the instructions for making the basic cracker described on pages 56-7 there is no reason why you should not use this pretty and decorative gift to enhance birthdays, christenings, wedding anniversaries and Easter Sunday.

IDEAS FOR FILLINGS

The filling you decide to use is really only limited by its size, your pocket and your imagination. Small can often be very beautiful and sometimes quite expensive, too. The advantage of making your own crackers is that the gift can be carefully chosen to suit the recipient. For children at Christmas a visit to any store

THE MAGIC OF CHRISTMAS CRACKERS

that sells stocking fillers will provide lots of imaginative ideas, from interestingly-shaped rubbers and pencil sharpeners to metal puzzles and plastic whistles. Other Christmas fillers could include individually wrapped chocolates and sweets, handkerchiefs, soap, perfume, golf balls and tees, hair ornaments, dice, indoor fireworks and garden seeds.

CHILDREN PULLING A CRACKER
'The Graphic', 1878

For Easter, of course, small chocolate eggs are the ideal filling, although they should really be individually wrapped for appearance sake. Home-made sweets are a good alternative and children, who have probably already consumed half-a-dozen chocolate eggs, will be just as delighted to discover one of the little yellow chicks obtainable from shops specializing in cake decorations nestling inside their cracker. More expensive gifts may be required for birthdays and wedding anniversaries, while silver napkin rings, charms or teaspoons are just the right size for a christening cracker.

DECORATIONS

Whatever you choose to fill your cracker, however, remember that the wrapping itself is just as important, and this is where you can give full rein to your imagination.

Suitable decorations for Christmas crackers include silk ribbons and bows, fabric flowers, ready-made cake decorations and intriguing little wrapped parcels, such as the one used in the photograph opposite. Tiny fir cones can be used, too. Use an old, stiff paint brush to remove any loose debris and then spray with gold or silver paint. Little bells can be painted in the same way and attached to the cracker with a red satin bow.

This is also where children can help, particularly at Christmas. Small hands will find the crackers themselves far too fiddly to make, but armed with a pot of paste, a pair of scissors and a stack of last year's Christmas cards a five-year-old will be usefully occupied for hours making personalized gifts.

MAKING YOUR OWN CHRISTMAS CRACKERS

CRACKERS CAN BE MADE USING a small card tube as the central compartment, but to make a really professional cracker the tube should be formed using a flat piece of paper and card, which should be rolled round a special pair of metal or plastic cylinders called 'formers'. This is then secured with adhesive and 'pulled' in two places to form the ends of the cracker, which keeps the contents safely inside the central compartment. Work seated at a free-standing table with a chair opposite you to which you can secure the pulling cord. Tie your end of the cord to a roll of paper to make it easier to hold.

MATERIALS

To make a basic cracker 30cm (12in) long, 5cm (2in) in diameter, you will need a piece of thin card measuring about 50 x 37cm (20 x 15in) for the layout plan. Cracker component firms will supply the following items: pair of no 6 formers 25 x 5cm (10 x 2in) and 16.5 x 5cm (6½ x 2in) (or cut your own from plastic or aluminium tubing available from builders' merchants); crepe cracker papers 34 x 20cm (13½ x 8in) with crimped ends (or cut them from crepe paper, making sure the grain runs the length of the paper); stiffener cards 19 x 10cm (7½ x 4in) or lightweight card; lining papers 30 x 18cm (12 x 7in) (or thin typing paper); snaps; mottos; paper hats; and gold, silver or coloured banding to decorate. You will also need 1 metre (1 yard) of pulling cord – use waxed string or upholstery twine to avoid tearing the crepe paper; adhesive – paste-type glue is best; pinking shears and paper-cutting scissors.

METHOD

1. Draw the layout in pencil (*fig* 1).
2. Using a waterproof marking pen, clearly mark the guide lines and 'left' and 'right' on the formers (*fig* 2).
3. Lay a crimped paper on the layout against the 'left side of cracker' and 'lower side edge of cracker' lines (*fig* 3).
4. Cut strips of decorative banding 4-5 cm (1½ – 2in) wide by 20cm (8in) using pinking shears for a pretty edge. Glue the strips on to the paper using the spaced lines on the layout as a guide. Narrow strips 1cm (³⁄₈in) wide can be set just inside the crimped edge for extra decoration (*fig* 3). Turn the decorated paper over so the wrong side faces you.
5. Assemble the papers as shown in *fig* 4 using the cracker layout. Put the decorated cracker paper in place first with the wrong side facing you, lining it up with the 'left side of cracker' line and the 'lower side edge' line on the layout. Place the lining paper on top of the cracker paper. Put the snap and the motto in position as shown. Place the stiffener card on top, lining it up with the guide lines on the layout. Secure the stiffener and the lining paper with a spot of glue. This helps to keep the papers in position when several crackers are being prepared at one time.
6. Position the two formers two thirds down the cracker paper to make a continuous tube (*fig* 4). Paste a line of glue along the top edge of the paper. Holding the formers against the edge of the stiffener paper with one hand, lift up the near edge of the papers and roll them away from you, working them round the formers as tightly as possible. Keep the formers snugly in position. Make sure the edges of the cracker stick well

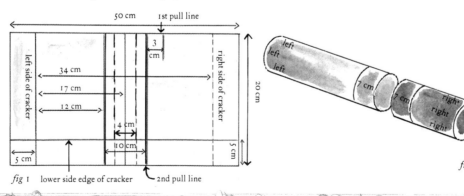

fig 1   lower side edge of cracker   2nd pull line

50 cm   1st pull line
left side of cracker
right side of cracker
34 cm
17 cm
12 cm
4 cm
10 cm
5 cm
5 cm
20 cm
3 cm

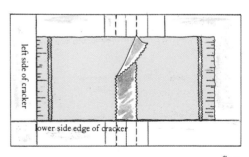

fig 2

fig 3

left side of cracker
lower side edge of cracker

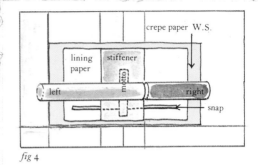

fig 4

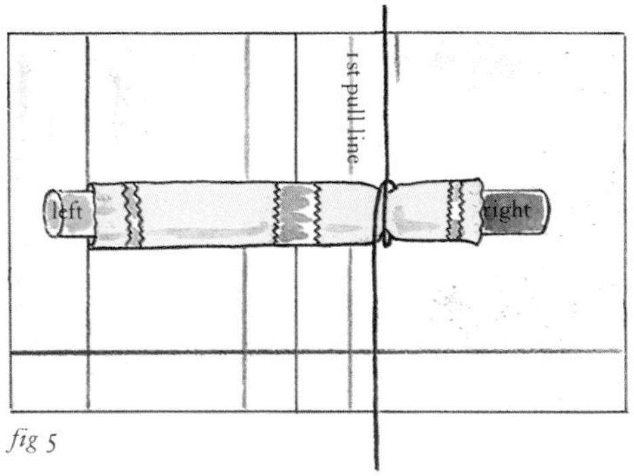

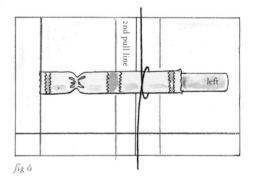

fig 5

fig 6

together by holding it firmly for a few minutes.

7. Holding both formers in place with your left hand, place the pulling cord over the cracker with your right and pass it round loosely once. Put the cracker towards the top of the layout plan in line with the 'left side of cracker' line and the cord exactly over the '1st pull' line.

Gently ease out the right-hand former until its red guide line is visible, no farther. Pull the cord tightly with the right hand, keeping the cracker straight and the cord at right angles to it (fig 5). The cord should be pulled with equal strength from both sides of the table.

8. Press the formers together again and give them a little twist. This gives the 'pull' a crisp look. Unwind the cord and remove only the right hand former.

9. Hold the cracker upright in your left hand and drop in the gifts. Make sure that they have dropped right down into the centre without sticking inside the left hand former.

10. Replace the cracker on the layout plan as shown in fig 6. Wind the cord round the cracker, aligning it with the second pull line. Gently ease out the former as far as the red guide line. Place the cord centrally between the former and the stiffener board. Pull the cord to make the second pull and twist gently as before. Slip the former out.

If you are putting frills on the crackers, now is the time to add them. One cracker paper will make the frills for both ends of a cracker. Cut in two as shown in fig 7, discarding the central strip. Fold both pieces together and snip zigzags on both edges (fig 8). Separate the papers and fold each one so that one cut edge reaches the crimping. Dot each 'V' with glue. Sprinkle on glitter, shake off excess and leave to dry. Insert a fine knitting needle in the fold and gather it as shown in fig 9. Slip out the needle and press the paper along the fold line to hold the gathering firm. Cut a 20cm (8in) piece of shirring elastic; stretch it, and insert inside the folded edge. Put the

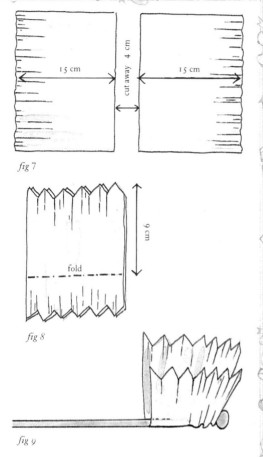

fig 7

fig 8

fig 9

frill on top of the cracker and tie it at the back of the 'pull', as tightly as you can without breaking the elastic. Trim the ends of the elastic. Fluff up the frills by pulling each one slightly from its base.

To Decorate

Choose suitable decorations with an eye to the overall colour scheme. Gold or silver paint works well with cones or bells, and ribbons can be in matching or contrasting colours. Fix them with a good quick-drying adhesive and/or small piece of double-sided sellotape.

CHRISTMAS FARE HAS ALWAYS included nuts, fruit, sweets, cakes and biscuits. Gingerbread men and animals are given as gifts in many countries, and in Holland, Scandinavia and German-speaking countries special shaped and decorated biscuits are traditionally offered to guests, especially when they visit during Advent, the time leading up to Christmas, and on Christmas Eve.

These Christmas goodies not only taste delicious, but also make excellent tree decorations. If not left on the tree for too long, they can still be eaten. They tend to disappear quite quickly, but you can always re-furnish the tree with new supplies when your guests for the day have gone home, so that you have a continual store of small gifts. Some of the simpler recipes can also be made by the children; their pride in their own work may then help to keep little fingers from denuding the tree before time – always a temptation with edible decorations of any sort, especially when they look as good as they taste.

TASTY TREE DECORATIONS

TURRON/TORRONE

At Christmas children in Spain and Italy eat a nougat-like sweet called turron (torrone). Cut into squares and wrapped in coloured cellophane or foil this would make a very appropriate and pretty addition to the Christmas tree. Tie on with ribbon.

INGREDIENTS
100g (4oz) blanched and toasted almonds
100g (4oz) toasted hazelnuts
whites of 2 large eggs
100g (4oz) clear honey
100g (4oz) caster sugar

Beat egg whites until stiff. Chop nuts and mix with egg whites. Put sugar and honey in a saucepan and bring to the boil. Add nut mixture and cook over a moderate heat for 10 minutes, beating continually.

Turn the turron into a container lined with greaseproof paper, smooth it down and cover with more paper. Put a weight on top and leave to set for two days.

PRETZELS AND POPCORN

Use shop-bought pretzels to decorate your Christmas tree, sticking them together to create ever-more fanciful shapes. Use a frosting 'glue' made of egg white and icing sugar and, once stuck together, leave the new ornaments to dry for several hours on greaseproof paper before tying on the tree with ribbon or gold or silver cord. Handle them gently.

Popcorn, too, can be made into attractive tree decorations, and is now available in a range of amazing colours. If you buy your own corn to pop, follow the instructions on the side of the package – don't forget to put a lid on the pan, though, or you could end up knee-deep in popcorn!

Try hanging the tree, American-style, with strings of popcorn, sewn together with a needle and thread. You can either loop lengths of popcorn round the tree or make it into tiny wreaths and attach them to the tree, inconspicuously with the same thread or decoratively with a ribbon bow.

Decorated Biscuits

These biscuits, spiced or flavoured with aniseed or vanilla, come in a wide variety of different shapes and make delightful Christmas tree decorations.

Ingredients

100g (4oz) caster sugar
100g (4oz) unsalted butter
225g (8oz) plain flour, sifted
1/2 x 5ml (1/2 teaspoon) cinnamon
pinch of ginger
1 small egg, beaten

Cream sugar and butter together, add the egg, stir in the flour and spices and mix until you get a firm dough. If you have time put the dough in the fridge for an hour or two; this does improve it but is not strictly necessary.

Set the oven to 190°C (375°F or Gas Mark 5). Roll the dough out gently until it is fairly thin and cut into shapes, either with a sharp knife or with special biscuit cutters; holly-leaves with berries are easy to form; Christmas shapes such as Father Christmas, a star, a bell and a Christmas tree are available. Moon shapes and initials are also very attractive but remember that the simpler the shape the less likely it is to crumble or break.

You also need room to make the hole if you are using the biscuits as decorations: use a skewer to make a neat hole near the top of each biscuit. (If it closes up during cooking, re open it gently with the point of the skewer.)

Place the shapes carefully on a greased and floured baking sheet and cook near the top of the oven for about 10 minutes; keep a close eye on them as they don't take long to overcook. Leave on the sheet for a few minutes when you take them out, then cool on a wire rack.

To Decorate

Decorate in any way you wish, according to taste and to what you have in store.

* Dip all or half the biscuit into melted plain chocolate and leave to cool or sprinkle with hundreds and thousands. Press on chopped nuts or glacé cherries.

* Cover with white glacé icing and stud with silver balls, jelly sweets or cake decorating flowers.

* Pipe on children's initials in icing flavoured with almond essence or lemon.

Thread ribbon or fine gold cord through the holes to hang the biscuits on the Christmas tree.

ALTHOUGH IN SOME COUNTRIES, Germany for instance, the Christmas tree is traditionally decorated in secret and only revealed to the children in all its glory on Christmas Eve, children do love to help with the dressing of their tree and get such fun from actually making the decorations that it is a pity to deny them this pleasure.

The tree ornaments we describe here are not difficult to make; there is something to suit every level of ability. Nor are they expensive so you don't have to worry about wasted materials if things go wrong. Most of the ideas are just suggestions that can be adapted to your own taste and according to the materials you may have available.

PAPER FANS

Cut a strip of coloured tissue paper 23 x 7.5cm (9 x 3in) with pinking shears and pleat it widthways. Stitch the pleats together at one end with needle and thread or bind with sticky-backed foil. Open out the fan and tie to the tree with matching gold or silver cord.

TREE DECORATIONS FOR CHILDREN TO MAKE

FELT STOCKINGS

Cut out the shapes shown and oversew the edges together with thread of a contrasting colour. Decorate with scraps of lace, sequins, glass beads or ric-rac, sewn or glued on as appropriate. Make a loop of matching cotton at the top back of the stocking to hang it.

TOY DRUMS

Cut 5cm (2 in) sections from kitchen or toilet-paper roll tubes and cover with red crepe paper, foil or shiny coloured paper. Decorate the drum with zigzags of silver cord and trim with blue and silver dressmaking braid or ric-rac. Use more cord to hang the drum on the tree.

CHRISTMAS PARCELS

Cover pillboxes or half-matchboxes with Christmas wrapping-paper and tie with gold or silver cord, making a loop for hanging on the tree.

NET POMPOMS

Cut stiff net fabric into 1.5cm (½in) strips and thread through a pair of cardboard shapes placed together – on the same principle as woolly pompoms. Continue until the centre hole is filled and the circles completely covered.

Gently cut the net edges between the two circles and tie tightly round the net thus revealed. Slide off the circles and fluff out the ball. Lightly touch the outside of the ball with glue and roll in glitter. Knock off any excess and sew a ribbon on for hanging to the tree.

LANTERNS

Simple lanterns are even easier to make if you use sticky-backed paper or foil. Fold a 7.5cm (3in) square of paper in half and cut into it from the fold as evenly as possible, leaving 6mm (¼in) uncut at the far edge and at each side.

Open out and stick the sides together. Make handles from paper strips of a different colour and stick on.

DOUGH CUT-OUTS

(Note: these decorations are not edible.) Stir 5 x 15 ml (5 tablespoons) of cold water gradually into 150g (5 oz) plain flour and 15 ml (1 tablespoon) salt until the mixture becomes crumbly. Knead so that it leaves the sides of the bowl, adding extra flour or water as necessary. Knead the dough for 5 minutes more until pliable and roll out to about 6mm (¼ in) thickness.

Cut stars, bells, snowmen or holly wreaths, embellishing them with hand-rolled strips and balls. Make a hole at the top to hang a cord through. Cook on a baking sheet at 130°C (250°F or Gas Mark ½) until hard and dry (about 40 minutes).

When cool, colour with enamel or poster paints.

PADDED TREE

Cut two tree shapes from Christmas fabric 10cm (4in) by 10cm (4in) by 8cm (3¼in) and stitch, wrong sides together, leaving a small opening in the short edge. Turn inside out and stuff with cottonwool or kapok.

Make the trunk with two 2.5cm (1in) squares of red fabric, seamed with wrong sides together, turned out and stuffed. Insert trunk into tree opening and sew in place. Thread red silk or wool through top of tree to hang.

DRESSING YOUR TREE

How you dress the tree can be as important as what you dress it with. Hurling on all your assembled baubles any-old-how is unlikely to result in an attractive finished product, even though when you are working with children and their contributions you are more likely to be settling for a generally colourful effect than stylized elegance.

Whether you've opted for a real or an artificial tree, it's a good idea to match it and its decoration to the theme or style you've chosen for the rest of your house. Don't, for example, go for a very modern and subtle look for your tree if you've plumped for angels and cribs, and boughs of holly, ivy and mistletoe elsewhere. Remember to extend the theme when you come to disguise the pot or tub in which the tree is anchored.

You don't necessarily have to choose a real tree – spruce, fir or pine – to create a traditional mood, as there are many good 'look-alike' fake trees on the market. It's also true that red and green, colours particularly associated with the Christmas season, can be used to stunning effect on a silver or gold tinsel tree.

Begin by making sure that your Christmas tree is upright and completely secure; it is heartbreaking to dress the tree only to have the weight of the decorations or a wobbly table cause it to topple over, breaking baubles and, even more irritating, damaging the so-sensitive Christmas light wiring.

Most artificial trees come with their own stand. If you have a real tree, wedge the stump into a pot with half-bricks and fill up with damp sand, both for steadiness and to help delay the dropping of the tree's needles. (Spraying with a special anti-desiccant will also help.) Before you put on the decorations is also the time to use a fire-retardant spray and to cover the tub with Christmas wrapping-paper. Choose the latter to complement the scheme of your tree.

Put the lights on first, draping them right around the tree, working from top to bottom. Check that they are working properly *before* you put them on and don't bury them under other decorations in case they overheat.

Add the rest of your decorations with care, distributing them as evenly as possible over the whole tree – not just the front. Put the heavier items, such as the larger dough shapes, on first, making sure that they are positioned on the stronger branches and towards the centre of the tree. Leave the tips of the branches for tinsel or ultra-light ribbon or paper ornaments.

Think about following a colour theme for your Christmas tree, silver and red or all-gold for example – if this is possible with the variety of your children's offerings to accommodate! You could of course give them a theme in advance and make the decorations with that in mind – and not only a colour theme, but a *type* of ornament too.

If you intend to add further items at a later stage, for instance decorative biscuits, or gifts for a particular day's visitors, consider at this point where you might put them and allow for them on the tree. Alternatively, some of the Christmas tree decorations described on the previous pages can be converted into holders for presents, especially if slightly larger versions are made, for example the felt stocking. The drum needs only to have one open side covered with foil or crepe paper and to be hung so this becomes the bottom to serve as a container for nuts and dried fruit, sugared almonds or tiny gifts.

MISTLETOE

PICK A BERRY OFF THE MISTLETOE
FOR EV'RY KISS THAT'S GIVEN.
WHEN THE BERRIES HAVE ALL GONE,
THERE'S AN END TO KISSING.

CHRISTMAS JUST WOULDN'T BE Christmas without a tree as its centrepiece. Whether you choose real or fake, decorate it to look modern or traditional, dress it up to be elegant or jolly, it's an essential in any home.

The tradition in some European countries is for the adults of the household to dress the tree secretly, and then to reveal it, in all its splendour, to the children. While this can be a tremendous thrill for the young ones, it is also great fun to let them in on the act, making the occasion a special family treat.

During the weeks that lead up to Christmas, encourage the children to get started on the decorations which will eventually adorn the tree (see pages 60-1). When Christmas Eve comes round, if eager helpers can contain their impatience until then, assemble everything you want to put on the tree, then follow the guidelines opposite for the most sensible way to proceed. In order to include all the childrens' contributions, you will probably have to sacrifice any plans for a sophisticated design but, as our picture (right) shows, different colours, shapes and sizes can be teamed very successfully. The traditional Christmas colours of red, green and gold are used, but with splashes of more unexpected shades, such as the bright blue of the baubles clustered at the top of the tree and the orange of the pretty paper fans. The forest green of a real tree makes a perfect subdued backdrop for this multi-coloured mixture.

As a safety precaution always switch off the Christmas tree lights at night or if you go out for any length of time.

For many people, a Christmas tree should be a mass of bright baubles, twinkling fairy lights and shimmering garlands of tinsel – this is the season of over-indulgence, after all! For a change however, you may like to consider some of the following ideas.

An old-fashioned, but very charming way of decking out your tree is to drape it with home-made biscuits, sweets and marzipan fruits, wrapped prettily in coloured foil or cellophane. Add some nuts and pieces of fruit, such as seasonal tangerines and satsumas, and a few strands of tinsel or some coloured baubles, and your 'edible tree' will provide a small gift for all your Christmas visitors. Take care that your stock is not depleted at too early a stage of the festivities, though!

While red and green are the most typical Christmas colours, don't feel obliged to limit yourself to them if you wish to achieve a traditional effect. For our picture (on the left) we used white silk flowers all over the tree, and topped it with a luxurious bow in matching silk for a sumptuous and elegant finish. Candle-like fairy lights spread a warm and welcoming glow. Spare flowers – or, indeed, any other suitable tree decoration – can be used to put the finishing touches to prettily wrapped gifts.

A single motif repeated all over can look very impressive, such as generous bows, made from red, white, gold or orange ribbon, tied to the end of each

This attractively decorated Christmas tree is festooned with white silk flowers and topped with a matching white satin bow

branch; simple shapes, such as stars or bells, made from gold or silver card; felt stockings hung out ready for Father Christmas; or Christmas parcels (see page 60) made in just one or two colours to mirror the – hopefully huge – mound of presents nestling at the foot of the tree.

Single colour schemes for decorations are particularly effective when used on tinsel trees in bold shades. In general, the brighter the tree, the more subtle and understated you should make your decorations. It goes almost without saying that you should select this type of tree carefully, to avoid clashes with the colour scheme of your room.

Don't feel restricted to one type of decoration; baubles, tinsel, lights and so on can all be teamed successfully, without looking like a fairground, if you stick to the same, or a similar or co-ordinating, colour. Each bauble could be held in place with a length of matching ribbon, for example, in the colour of your choice. Decorations of the same shape, size and colour give a very up-to-the-minute effect.

Candles are sometimes still used in Germanic and Scandinavian countries. Although they give a lovely, inviting glow when lit, fire precautions should be strictly observed; perhaps candles are better saved for use as table decorations or in still life arrangements, where they are still attractive, but are much safer. Fairy lights make an excellent substitute, especially if you choose small, all-white lights or those that are candle-shaped.

A charming effect achieved with the most traditional of decorations – miniature wooden toys are teamed with bright red bows and presents are co-ordinated, too

'HEIGH-HO! SING, HEIGH-HO! UNTO the green holly' Shakespeare invited us in *As You Like It*. Indeed people had been singing the praises of holly and other evergreens for centuries before this, and still, at Christmas, we know of no more attractive way to decorate our homes.

The designs described here are built on wire frames covered with sphagnum moss which you can buy from a florist. Dry and clean to handle, it makes a natural cushion for the greenery and it doesn't matter if some shows through. There is no need to dampen the moss – this might damage a wooden surface. Instead cut the shrub stems diagonally, slit the ends and scrape them of bark, then stand them in water for two or three days before you start work. Do this and your greenery will easily last the Twelve Days of Christmas.

Deck the halls with boughs of holly,
'Tis the season to be jolly.
Don we now our gay apparel
Troll the ancient Yuletide carol.

See the blazing Yule before us,
Strike the harp and join the chorus,
Follow me in merry measure,
While I tell of Yuletide treasure.

Fast away the old year passes,
Hail the new ye lads and lasses,
Sing we joyous altogether,
Heedless of the wind and weather.

TRADITIONAL EVERGREEN WREATHS AND RINGS

THE ADVENT WREATH
Light a candle each Sunday of Advent, until all four are burning on the fourth Sunday. A traditional wreath, complete with moss and evergreen trimmings, cones, apples and ribbons

ADVENT WREATH

The Advent wreath is a hoop of evergreens and fruit bearing four candles, one of which is lit each week of Advent until all four are alight.

To make it, start, as for the kissing ring, by covering a wire frame with moss – all round the frame for a hanging design, on the top only if it is to be free-standing.

Position the candles first, equidistant around the ring. Bind thick wire round them and bend it underneath, wrap it several times around the base and secure the ends firmly. Cover the base with short sprays of evergreen needles such as juniper and yew then add holly or ivy to contrast.

Decorate with clusters of wired cones (see page 67), bunches of acorns, or dried seedheads – poppy or love-in-a-mist for example. For a hanging design, tie on small rosy apples with short lengths of narrow ribbon.

To hang the wreath, tie on four equal lengths of 5cm (2in) wide ribbon, evenly spaced between the candles. Staple the ends of the ribbons together – be sure they're all the same length or the wreath will not hang straight. This is particularly important if you wish to avoid hot wax dripping over furniture, carpets and people once the candles are lit.

Make a wire loop for the top and tie on a bow to decorate it, and smaller bows where the ribbons are fixed to the wreath. Once the wreath is in place, tie holly or mistletoe round the topmost bow. (For the free-standing design, wire on ribbon bows between the candles.)

type if possible, laurel and spotted laurel, bay and camellia. Wire these stems over the base in thick clusters.

Select a few gnarled and knobby twigs such as those of apple or pear and bind them on to the ring so they stray out from the edge. Wire on bunches of mistletoe or more shiny evergreens to fill any gaps. Last, wire a large ribbon bow to the top of the ring and make a loop with wire for hanging.

To wire cones and lichen, choose well-shaped undamaged cones. Wind 0.9mm (20 gauge) wire round the cone above the lowest layer of scales (or push it through the lichen). Bring the two ends together and twist tightly.

WELCOME RING

The delightful custom of hanging a circlet of evergreens, pine cones, nuts and twigs on the front door sprang up in Scandinavia. The design given here is simple to make.

Start with a 30cm (12 in) wire frame, bought or home-made, covered with tightly packed handfuls of moss bound on with fine wire. Cut short sprays of thick spiny evergreens such as juniper, cupressus, yew or fir and bind them on top of the moss, the stems all in one direction. Don't make this layer too dense.

Wire a dozen or so large cones (see below) and pieces of lichen. Push the wire ends through the evergreens and into the base, grouping the cones in clusters of two or three.

Cut short sprays of shiny evergreens that will contrast well with the base layer – ivy complete with shiny black berries, holly, including some of the variegated

KISSING RING

Mistletoe is the vital ingredient of a traditional kissing ring. Its associations with kissing, which have persisted in Britain into the twentieth century, may stem from its old link with fertility,

The kissing ring is easily built up on a wire coathanger base.

one of the many powers with which it is credited. It has always been held to be a pagan plant, and some of its other attributes include the power of healing, the ability to banish evil spirits, combat poisons, and to safeguard the home from thunder and lightning.

To make an old-fashioned kissing ring, bend two wire coathangers into circles and bend the hook of one so it matches the other. Use stub wire to bind the circles firmly together, criss-crossed to outline a sphere. Pack handfuls of moss tightly round the frame, binding it with a roll of wire. Bind short sprays of mixed evergreens, including mistletoe, to the frame, the leaves of each spray covering the stems of the one before. Tie a bunch of mistletoe with a ribbon, make a bow and tie it on beneath the frame. Tie a big floppy bow to the top of the frame.

THE HUMBLEST CHRISTMAS PRESENT deserves a pretty wrapping to transform it into something that looks exciting and enticing – and everyone is pleased to think that you have gone to extra trouble to make your gifts to them look extra special. The range of wrapping materials commercially available is vast and inspiring. The only limitation is likely to be the cost. Inspiration, however, costs nothing; and with a little time and thought some splendid parcels can be produced for the minimum outlay.

Think in terms of a collection of presents, of assorted sizes and shapes, but united by the colours in which they are wrapped. Limit yourself to no more than three colours, but don't dismiss the idea of sticking to just one: ice blue, for example, redolent of clear winter skies and frozen lakes. When you find a printed paper and accessories that you like, buy enough to wrap a few of your presents and supplement it with plain white lining paper, card, tape and ribbons, plus silver tinsel and stick on stars; write your cards with light blue ink.

PRACTICAL PACKING POINTS

Leave yourself plenty of time to do the job properly. Clear a sturdy working surface which will not be damaged by a stray blob of glue or scratched by scissors – and make sure you have everything you need to hand: boxes, paper, adhesive tape, ribbons, decorations, gift tags, coloured pens, tissue paper, shredded tissue, scissors and glue.

It is much simpler to wrap a solid square or oblong shape than to struggle with something either awkward, like a bottle, or soft, like a jumper. Make a

EXTRA-SPECIAL GIFT-WRAPPING IDEAS

habit of collecting empty boxes for presents like this, and pack breakable items in shredded tissue.

When wrapping objects which must stay the right way up, use a visual reminder of the top such as a bow. Place the item upside down on the wrapping paper so that once the edges are stuck together at the back the smooth right side will face up.

WRAPPING AND TRIMMING

The most important characteristic of a good-looking parcel is that it is neat. This means using the right size sheet of paper for the job, and of the right weight to fold smoothly. Thick heavy papers are unsuitable for tiny packages, for example. Foils with a high shine are difficult to fold at all; keep fixing them unobtrusively with little pieces of adhesive tape. Enormous presents may need two sheets of paper taped together – or take the easy way out and put them in a snowy white pillowcase tied at the neck with an opulent red ribbon.

Secure folded edges with the smallest practical piece of adhesive – or, better still, double-sided – tape. Tie up with ribbon and fix with a bow or a knot concealed with a separate bow before attaching trimmings. Here is a major opportunity to be inventive, with Christmas tree decorations, tinsel, silk or dried flowers, sprigs of seasonal greenery or berries, cake decorations, silver doilies – anything, in fact, that pleases your eye. Keep a watch on the proportion of things. A large present looks silly with an insignificantly small bow – though the reverse is not always true. Sometimes a small box is the better for a ribbon which is slightly too wide for it.

Make the gift tags part of the trimming, choosing the cards for colour and pattern. Cut out suitable small pictures from old Christmas cards, make a hole with a punch and thread through some narrow ribbon.

IDEAS FOR CHILDREN

Children may need help in wrapping presents neatly, but even the youngest can give their gifts a personal touch by designing the paper. Plain lining paper from decorating shops is the basic material. Printing with potato cuts is easy. Cut a large potato in half and cut away one end to make a simple fir tree shape, the other a tub. Dip one end in red paint, the other in green, and print rows of trees in tubs on the paper or scatter them all over. When the paint is dry, dab clear-drying glue on to the clean sections of the paper and shake glitter on top. Tap off the excess into a saucer and use it again. For a smaller version of this pattern, use an eraser (see page 49).

EVERGREENS, PRESERVED LEAVES, nuts, berries, fruit and flowers can be arranged together in countless ways to make decorative garlands, swags and table centrepieces or just inserted into a discreet ring of plasticine to decorate a tall candlestick.

TABLE CENTREPIECE

Table centrepieces add the finishing touch to any festive table. They should be chosen to match your table setting and can be made to look as traditional or modern as you wish. For the Christmas table, surround candles with a selection of dried flowers and evergreens according to taste and to what is available. The design described here and illustrated on page 72 follows a pink-based colour scheme with pale pink candles and dainty pink dried rosebuds.

To make the centrepiece: First, make a base of foam, about 25 x 12cm (10 x 5 in) and 5cm (2 in) deep, in a shallow container such as a foil baking tray.

Push the candles into the foam, then make the side trails with wheat, oats, dried pink larkspur, furry hare's tail grass, silver 'curry plant' leaves, thin trails of cupressus and, closer in to the foam, rosebuds and pink and white dried everlasting flowers.

Fill in the front and back, covering the foam completely, with clumps of dried lichen, lichen-covered twigs, glycerined beech leaves, silver leaves, cupressus, juniper and snippings of gypsophila and honesty. Push stems of rosebuds, leaves, grasses and seedheads between the candles – but keep the stems short and watch the dried materials carefully because they catch fire easily.

EVERGREEN GARLANDS AND DECORATIONS

'CARVED' SWAG

In Regency times, Grinling Gibbons, the English sculptor and wood-carver, carved life-like designs in wood featuring exquisite fruit, nuts, flowers and leaves. Re-create his designs using plant materials with the look and feel of carved wood – cones, bunches of acorns, nuts such as walnuts and pecans and dried flower heads such as those of poppy, aquilegia, rue and spurge. Heads of dried cereals make good 'points' to extend the height and give wispy trails, and clumps of lichen are good fillers. Use skeletonized Chinese lantern heads and pale dried everlasting flowers as the 'flowers'.

For the evergreens choose leaves with an architectural feel such as spruce and fir and contrast them with shiny-berried ivy, holly and mistletoe. For contrast, and for its woody colouring, add glycerined beech and other leaves with an attractive colour or texture.

To make the swag: Use a shallow plastic trough with a handle (12 x 8cm, about 5 x 3 in, see *fig* 1) filled with a piece of dry foam cut to fit, and push all the plant stems into this, some cut very short, so that it is completely hidden. (You can also use the paper plait base of a string of garlic and bind the materials on with wire.)

To hold cones in place, wire them as described on page 67. To secure nuts, push on a dab of blue sticky clay and either press this so it sticks to other materials, or push a wire through it.

Tie a ribbon, chosen to complement the colours of the arrangement, to the top (see *fig* 2).

LEAFY GARLAND

There's a luxurious look about a room decorated with a ribbon of evergreens and dried flowers – hanging over a fireplace, outlining a door or archway, or pinned to the front of the cloth on a buffet table. Make the garland with all evergreens as for the Advent wreath (p. 66) or contrast glycerine-preserved beech leaves (available from florists) with cupressus or yew. Decorate this with small fruits such as apples or mandarins, clusters of holly berries, bunches of acorns, cones, seedheads such as those of love-in-a-mist, poppy or honesty, and dried flowers such as helipterum, ammobium and statice.

To make: For the hidden base make a long tube of 5cm (2 in) wide wire mesh, fill it with sphagnum moss and push in the plant stems or use a piece of the thickest string or clothes-line cord and bind on a covering of moss. Wire the base evergreens to this with roll wire, and then add the decorations.

Measure the area to be decorated, allowing for generous loops, and cut the string and make a knot in the centre. Wire on the moss. Cut sprays of evergreens, about 7.5cm (3 in) long, and, working from the centre outwards, wire them on so the tips of one spray cover the stems of the next.

Wire on bunches or clusters of the decorations, making special features at the centre and other high points. Tuck in extra evergreens to fill any gaps. Fix securely to the wall or woodwork.

For a table cloth, keep the evergreen base light in both weight and appearance, and go for the more delicate materials such as everlasting flowers, dyed grasses, cream-faded Chinese lanterns and silver leaves (sage, limonium and 'curry plant') to decorate it.

THE POWERS OF EVERGREENS

BAY
Bay is an ancient symbol of power, used for the wreaths of Roman heroes.

HOLLY
Holly is thought to represent the drops of blood which fell from Christ's crown of thorns. It protects against witches.

IVY
Ivy is a pagan plant, associated with Bacchus, the god of revelry, and thought to protect against drunkenness.

LAUREL
Laurel is a cleanser and protector. It symbolizes victory and honour.

MISTLETOE
Mistletoe was the sacred plant of the Druids and is held to promote fertility and peace, and protect from evil spirits.

ROSEMARY
Rosemary is the plant of friendship and remembrance. It was the most common garnish for the boar's head.

YEW
Yew is poisonous to man, but is reputed to be a good defence against witches.

CHRISTMAS DINNER IS PROBABLY THE highlight of the gastronomic calendar. There is no question that it merits a very special table setting, not only because it is a great festival but also because it is the occasion for some time-honoured rituals.

Whether your gathering is for four people or fourteen, a large table looks impressive and is eminently practical, considering that it must accommodate an unusual number of plates, glasses, serving dishes and spoons, as well as wine bottles or a decanter, space to carve a turkey and enough room for your guests to feel comfortable as they linger over the last mouthfuls of Christmas pudding and brandy butter. If there was ever a time to display a fine polished dining table to advantage, this is it, taking care that there are enough heatproof mats to protect it. If you do not have a large enough table, do not despair. Use a sideboard or a supplementary table to cope with the extra dishes. As long as it's steady any table will do: cover both it and the dining table with matching cloths and they'll look like a pair, especially if you link them with similar flower arrangements or other decorations.

Just as people have expectations about the Christmas menu, so are there other elements without which it simply wouldn't be Christmas. Foremost among these are crackers. Every guest must have one, and if you make your own (see pages 56-7) their splendour may rival the turkey. Candles are another feature particularly appropriate to this meal, whether slender scarlet tapers in silver candelabra or a cluster of lowly nightlights gathered in the centre of the table.

SETTING A FESTIVE TABLE

A beautiful table setting takes time to prepare. Aim to complete laying the table on Christmas morning, if not making a start the night before. When your guests arrive, you want them to be enchanted by the sight of it – starched linen, gleaming glasses and all.

THE TRADITIONAL TABLE

What more traditional setting could there be than a snowy white damask cloth set with silver and crystal, with a centrepiece of holly and red candles, green and red crackers at each place? The secret here (though it is no less essential whatever style you choose) is that everything is perfect: not a knife or glass out of line, everything polished mirror-bright, the candles straight as soldiers in the centre. Staying with the formal approach does not mean sticking to tradition, however, for it is easy to vary the colour scheme without losing the seasonal spirit. Dusky pink, pale grey or antique gold cloths and napkins can supply an equally sumptuous background for the meal of the year. Rosebuds provide the inspiration for the shapely centrepiece shown here, candles enhancing its warm glow.

THERE ARE MANY REASONS WHY, though you wouldn't dream of not celebrating Christmas, you want to do it your way, breaking with tradition when you design your table. One of the most effective ways of doing this is to dispense with colour entirely (leaving your guests and the food itself to provide stimulation on that front) and stick to white: frosty, immaculate and very impressive. In the setting shown below, a great variety of textures has been used: clear shining crystal and silver, crisp linen, velvety flowers and softly gleaming candlelight combine to give a dramatic effect.

A BREAK WITH TRADITION

Still working on the lines of a single colour, be bold with red, which may have its place in the tried and tested Christmas spectrum but is not often used bravely enough, on table-cloth, napkins, candles, flowers, crackers … and wine!

A modern approach with its origins firmly in the past and which can readily be interpreted for a family dinner is the rustic look. Set a scrubbed pine table with earthenware dishes and make several small arrangements of dried flowers and grasses with beeswax candles in wooden holders. Use cream-coloured woven linen napkins.

For many people the arrival of the first Christmas card marks the start of Christmas and it is often tempting just to pop cards up on the nearest shelf or mantelpiece where they gather dust and get in the way, falling over every time someone reaches for a book or slams the door. This of course presupposes that your home has window sills and mantelpieces at all – so many modern houses and flats simply do not.

A properly organized display of Christmas cards not only solves these problems but makes a positive decorative feature of one of our friendliest customs.

DISPLAYING CHRISTMAS CARDS WITH STYLE

SWAGS AND GARLANDS
Hang the cards on, or clip or tie the cards to, lengths of fine string slung across the walls so that the string is completely covered, or make a V-shape by the same method, perhaps highlighting a centrally placed picture or wall ornament.

Punch a hole in the back of the card and fasten it to the string with a bag closure twist or use tiny plastic pegs or coloured paper clips. You will need a fairly secure anchorage for the string, preferably into wood.

VERTICAL STRIPS
Hang vertical strips of sellotape, sticky side out, and stick the cards on to this. A cross-piece of masking tape should hold it firm at the top.

Use brightly coloured ribbon in the same way, tying or stapling cards on and leaving enough room occasionally to stick on a ribbon rosette between the cards. Make a bow for the top and leave the bottom of the ribbon free, snipping

the end into an inverted V. Or top the ribbon strip with a giant sprig of holly. Attaching the cards with ribbon threaded through the top left-hand corner is an extravagant use of ribbon but resplendently effective.

STAR SHAPE
Make an impact with a big star shape of cards on an otherwise empty stretch of wall. Use sellotape, sticky side out, or string and clips as described above. Graduate the cards so that larger ones are at the centre and smaller ones at the points.

With a big arrangement such as this beware of ruining your paint or wallpaper; try to attach your support to woodwork if possible.

FLOATING BALLOONS
An extravagant solution for a home with high ceilings: attach strings of Christmas cards to helium-filled balloons. The silver ones are attractive in themselves, they rise naturally right up to the ceiling

and should last out the Christmas season before losing their buoyancy.

A CARD TREE
If you have room, spray or paint bare winter branches with white, silver or gold and arrange them in a large vase. Hang them with a selection of your smaller cards and add a few tiny baubles and fine threads of tinsel for a really striking display feature.

IN THE HALL
Cards hung from the banisters will move slightly in any movement of air. If strung on the wall beside the stairs they can be seen as you go up and down.

For the stairwell, or anywhere else you have the headroom, make a 'mobile' of Christmas cards. Use wire coathangers to make a circle from which to hang cards either in two or three solid tiers or randomly at different lengths.

Bind the ring with coloured crepe paper or ribbon and suspend it by means of lengths of fine cord tied on to a small central ring – this is to ensure that your main ring hangs level. You will need a well-secured hook to take the weight.

ON THE SHELF
Where you do decide to make use of shelves and ledges to display Christmas cards, avoid later headaches: make space for the cards by clearing away some of your usual ornaments and dust thoroughly before you start to put them up. Position any cards sent specifically to the children at a low level so they don't knock the whole lot over when showing off their cards to friends. Choose shelves which aren't prone to every draught.

Festive
ENTERTAINMENT

All hail to the days that merit more praise
    Than all the rest of the year,
And welcome the nights that double delights
    As well for the poor as the peer!
Good fortune attend each merry man's friend
    That doth but the best that he may,
Forgetting old wrongs with carols and songs,
    To drive the cold winter away.

From *The Praise of Christmas*, by T. Durfey *et al*.

THEMES FOR A CHRISTMAS PARTY

Make your christmas party into something a bit out of the ordinary by following a theme, not just by asking your guests to dress up but by expressing your chosen theme in everything from the style and colour of the invitations right through to the food and, for children, the going-home presents. Since you will presumably already have put up Christmas decorations, you will not want to disturb them – or indeed to forget that it is Christmas; so go for something seasonal.

RED AND GREEN PARTY

These are of course traditional colours, embodied in the bright leaves of holly with its scarlet berries.

Send out tree-shaped invitations on stiff green card in red envelopes and ask everyone to dress in these colours, even if it means abandoning their usual party clothes for costumes: green might again mean a Christmas tree – graduated layers of gathered crepe paper sewn on to an old dress, and red for Santa Claus of course!

Add a few extra touches to the party room/s in the way of candles, crackers and paper hats. Cover the buffet table with a plain white cloth, slip red and green paper doilies under the serving dishes and scatter a handful of green and red sequins over the table.

You can really have fun with the food for a theme party. Italian food is attractively red and green – serve pizza and lasagne, pink and green tutti-frutti ice-cream, and for drinks chianti, campari or martini. Or make spinach quiche, smoked salmon sandwiches and asparagus rolls and decorate the table with tomato 'flowers'. Individual cherry tarts are easy to make and look very pretty.

Serve with appropriately coloured cocktails – grenadine or blackcurrant-based for the red and chartreuse-based for the green. Kir Royale, blackcurrant liqueur with champagne or sparkling white wine, is simple to cope with if you have a quantity to make, and the children will be thrilled to have their own non-alcoholic drink – Diabolo Menthe, fizzy lemonade with mint syrup.

Wrap party-game and going-home presents in shiny red or green foil paper. As an alternative for a stylish adult party, follow a gold and glitter theme.

MEDIEVAL BANQUET

Indulge all your fantasies of Christmas in 'Merrie England', even if they are not authentic! Ask your guests to come in costume: a tall pointed hat and a robe or a saucy wench neckline for ladies perhaps and a gold card crown and a pair of tights, 'hose', for the gentlemen if they are not up to anything more ambitious.

Ask an extrovert friend to dress up as a jester or act as Lord of Misrule and lead the party in fun and games. Play old favourites like Blind Man's Buff, Hunt the Thimble and now-forgotten games such as Hot Cockles (a blindfold player holds out his hand, cries 'Hot cockles, hot!' and receives a slap on it from another, whose name he must then guess) and get the Lord of Misrule to hand out forfeits to losers.

Get your guests in the mood with a wassail bowl of spiced ale floating with roasted apples or mulled wine or cider, and, for the buffet, spareribs in hot sauce, honey-coated chicken drumsticks and trays of hot garlic bread. They may not be remotely medieval – at Christmas time anyway – but do also provide some fresh green salads with sliced avocado, cucumber and lettuce. Syllabub makes a delicious – and authentic – dessert.

A Dickens Party

Hold a Victorian Christmas party with guests asked to come as characters from the works of Charles Dickens, the man who epitomizes the season of simple sentiment and jovial goodwill.

Play old parlour-games, and snap-dragon – snatching raisins from a dish of burning brandy – and serve cold beef and salads, mince pies, beer, fruit wines

and a hot punch. Find someone to play the piano and sing carols.

When it is time to go home give everyone a drawstring bag filled with sugared almonds or crystallized ginger.

Foreign Customs

Copy the customs of other lands. On 6th December, for instance, have a St Nicholas Day party for children featuring hot chocolate, sweet pastries and letter-shaped biscuits while the adults present drink bishop's punch (spiced sherry or port with hot water, lemons and sugar). Set the children to composing verses and riddles about one another and attach these to the going-home presents brought by St Nicholas himself – with Black Peter to scare those who haven't behaved! Or follow the custom of the German-speaking countries, by having friends round for a special Christmas Eve supper to light the final candle on the Advent wreath.

GETTING THE PARTY GOING

As we enter the season of good cheer and parties, hosts and hostesses will be especially keen to fulfil our expectations of jollity and make *their* party one that will be remembered.

Make a friendly welcome with a Christmas wreath on the front door or tie a big bunch of ribbons or balloons to the door or gate; this is also useful to those who are not familiar with the house.

The words 'fancy dress' or 'come as . . .' on an invitation not only increase the usual pre-party anticipation but get people ready to enjoy themselves right from the start – before they arrive indeed. What is more, fancy dress encourages people, once at the party, to mix well, released from some of their usual reserve simply by wearing something other than their habitual garb.

You can also avoid awkward clumps of silent guests by asking people to come to the party dressed up as one half of a well-known pair (for instance Beauty and the Beast, Ham and Eggs). Once arrived, they must seek out their other half and make themselves known.

For non-fancy-dress parties, tell new arrivals, randomly, that they are this or that half of a pair of famous lovers and leave them to discover who is the Olive Oyl to their Popeye or Antony to their Cleopatra, a good excuse to mix. If you are overburdened with men assign Snow White as many dwarves as necessary; if with women, try Henry VIII and his wives.

Tie a balloon to the ankle and wrist of everybody arriving at the party; this should lead to a few laughs as guests tussle with drinks and cigarettes – before the balloons burst!

Hang a kissing ring or just a big bunch of mistletoe in a central position to be taken advantage of as the situation demands. Forfeits might dictate that use be made of this!

As well as more intellectual pursuits such as charades and dumb crambo (see pages 84-5) organize guests into teams and have a relay version of an egg and spoon race using table tennis balls and dessert spoons. Or play 'cutting the chocolate': the players sit in a circle throwing dice in turn until someone throws a six. This person then dons a couple of items intended both to hinder his movements and to look ridiculous (for instance motorcycle gauntlets and a big sunhat or a baby's plastic bib) before setting to and eating as much chocolate as possible from a large bar using an ordinary knife and fork. The player continues until someone else throws a six – it is then this person's turn. Strictly for fans of chocolate but great fun.

Make a talking point of the buffet as well as saving yourself a lot of washing-up and worry about breakages by using all disposable tableware. Plates, bowls, cutlery, napkins, tablecloths and even glasses can be bought in a variety of subtle and striking shades. Use two toning or contrasting colours and enhance the effect with party streamers. Add a selection of blowers, shakers and

balloons and fill bowls with sweets.

Finally, give a Christmassy touch to the spread with massed candles.

NEW YEAR'S EVE

If you are holding a New Year's Eve party be sure to maintain the momentum of the party after the celebrations of midnight. Introduce a fresh idea if possible, for instance producing horoscopes for the coming year for all the guests to read and compare.

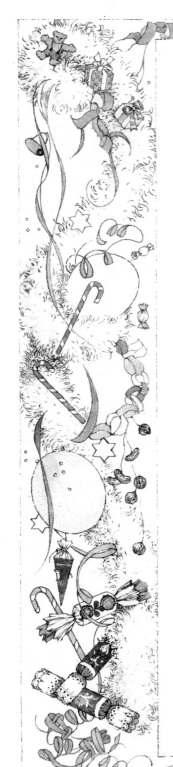

GAMES FOR ALL THE FAMILY

TODAY CHRISTMAS IS OFTEN THE only time when all the members of a family have the opportunity to get together in the mood to make their own entertainment and play games. In previous centuries this was much more usual; the Victorians in particular devised many parlour games. The games suggested here can be played by all the family and simplified or made more difficult according to the ages of those taking part. They are not really competitive games; the fun is in the taking part rather than in winning.

FLIP THE KIPPER

You can play this game with as many people as can line up across your sitting-room or work in teams. Cut each player a paper fish shape about 24 x 15cm (10 x 6 in) and decorate each differently or mark with their names; everyone can join in doing this first if you want.

The idea of the game is to race the kippers to the far end of the room by whacking on the ground behind your kipper with a rolled-up newspaper so that it flaps and flies along. Easy as it sounds, it takes a certain knack, and it may be the youngest player who wins.

SAUSAGES

This is another game to get everyone laughing; just describing it gets children going! One person is the questioner. He asks each player a question in turn; whatever he asks, the answer must always be 'Sausages'. If the person questioned forgets to answer 'Sausages' or laughs then he changes places with the questioner and the game starts again.

FIZZ-BUZZ

A game for older children and adults, Fizz-Buzz needs quick thinking and is best when played fast. Count round in a circle, substituting 'Fizz' for the number 5, any number with 5 in it or divisible by 5, and 'Buzz' for number 7, any number with 7 in it or divisible by 7.

THE VICAR'S CAT

This is a Victorian word game. Each player in turn has to find an adjective to describe the Vicar's cat, first adjectives starting with the letter A (The Vicar's cat is agile/angry for example) and going on to Z (The Vicar's cat is zestful/zealous). You can either ask every player to find an 'A' adjective before going on to 'B' or have the first person doing 'A', the second 'B' and so on.

PASS THE ORANGE

This pair of games suits all ages; seeing young and old engaged in them together makes them even more amusing. Divide into two teams, standing in rows. The first person in each line tucks an orange under his chin and tries to pass it to the next in line in the same way without either of them using their hands. The first team to get the orange to the end without dropping it wins the game. If you drop the orange you have to start again from the beginning.

This game can also be played using a balloon, but in this case, hold it between your knees. Players must not drop or burst the balloon.

CONSEQUENCES

An old favourite for players who can read and write. Write a man's name at the top of a sheet of paper; fold the paper so you can't read the name and pass it to the person on your left. Next write a woman's name, then where they met, what he said to her, what she to him, what he gave her and she gave him, what the consequences were, and lastly what the world said, passing on the sheets of paper after each addition to the story.

Then each person in turn reads out the sheet they hold, unfolding it as they read. The fun comes from the ridiculous juxtapositions brought about by the jumbling of the stories.

WINNING AND LOSING

Where there are winners, let them dip into a bran tub of prettily wrapped small gifts. (You can buy bran for this from pet shops.) You may feel that good losers deserve something too!

Write forfeits on to cards and let losing players of any game choose one. Forfeits might include having to sing a song, dance a jig, spell a tricky word, kiss another guest or answer riddles.

BLIND MAN'S BUFF
by Kate Greenaway

PARLOUR GAMES FOR ADULTS

WITH THE RENEWED POPULARITY of mime and word games on television in recent years, more and more people are willing to drop their 'sophisticated' front and allow themselves the pleasant indulgence of playing games at home or with friends. Before the days of television of course no-one denied themself this fun and most of the games described here have truly stood the test of time.

DUMB CRAMBO

A rhyming game, this goes back at least as far as the seventeenth century; Pepys mentions it in his diaries.

Choose two teams and ask Team 1 to leave the room. Team 2 chooses a word then sends a member out to tell Team 1 a word that rhymes with the one they have chosen, for example 'cat' if they have chosen 'sat'.

Team 1 returns and mimes the word they think might be the chosen one, perhaps trying 'mat'. As this is wrong they are hissed (no-one is allowed to speak) and have to try again. Points are given for guessing the correct word.

When Team 1 guesses the correct word, Team 2 claps, then takes its turn in the other role. The team that gains most points wins.

ADVERBS

Another word game which involves miming. Send one player out of the room then choose any adverb and call the player back to guess what it is. He does this by asking the other players to perform some particular action in the manner of the adverb, for example 'Eat your dinner in this manner', 'Talk in this manner', so if the adverb were 'stiffly' the actors must pretend to eat and talk stiffly until the player guessing hits upon the correct adverb. You can limit him to a set number of guesses if you wish.

DEFINITIONS

Choose a question master and supply him with a good dictionary from which he picks out and reads the definition of a word. The other players have to try and guess what word the definition fits.

Alternatively, the question master can read out several definitions and then give one word (i.e. a word that one of these definitions describes) and the players have to choose which definition applies to that word. The player who gets most definitions correct is the winner.

Like most of these word games, Definitions can be pitched at a level to suit the ability and state of concentration of those taking part. It's no fun if they are too easy but not everyone feels like Einstein after Christmas dinner or a couple of glasses of wine.

MURDER

This brain-teaser is great fun but can be quite scary; don't let it get out of hand, especially if some of the company are of a nervous turn of mind!

From a pack of cards take the same number of cards as there are players, one being a jack and another an ace. Deal the cards out: whoever draws the ace is the Detective, whoever draws the jack is the Murderer (only the Detective identifies himself).

Leaving the Detective in the one lit room, the players move quietly around the dark house until the Murderer chooses a victim. Coming from behind, he touches the victim on the shoulder (round the neck for those with strong nerves!) whereupon the victim has to wait 10 seconds before calling out and collapsing. (The Murderer uses this time to move well away.)

All the other players have to stay where they are when the victim cries out. The Detective puts on the lights and questions them to find out who is the Murderer by asking who was where, when. Everyone but the Murderer has to tell the truth. When he thinks he has worked out who could have done the murder, the Detective makes his accusation. If he correctly accuses the Murderer, the villain must confess. If the Detective accuses the wrong person, the Murderer goes free.

CHARADES

Divide into teams and take turns to mime, syllable by syllable, a word, or, word by word, a book, film or song title or a well-known expression or saying, finally miming the whole subject of the charade, for example dividing up honey/moon or making mosquito into moss/key/toe. The team performing the charade can be asked whether it is one word or, if a phrase, how many words it contains.

Dressing up to perform the charade adds an extra dimension to the game and makes it even more amusing.

MUSICAL CHAIRS
Amusing to everyone except the stout gentleman on the floor

LAMB'S WOOLL

6 medium sized baked apples
1.2 litres (2 pints) ale
4 x 15ml (4 tablespoons) soft
brown sugar
½ x 5ml (½ teaspoon)
ground ginger
½ x 5ml (½ teaspoon)
grated nutmeg

Cut up the apples and put in a large bowl. Heat ale gently in a pan and pour over the apples. Add sugar and spices and leave somewhere warm for an hour. Strain through sieve back into saucepan and reheat gently.

Alternatively, warm the ale gently with the sugar and spices and just add the baked apples, whole, shortly before serving.

HOT DRINKS
FOR
COLD DAYS

I N THE COLD DAYS OF MIDWINTER alcoholic drinks which are served warm are always welcome. This would certainly have applied in those days, long before the invention of central heating when wassailers, carol-singers and Hogmanay toasters trudged from farm to farm or took to the streets for their celebrations, and needed something warming to keep up their spirits.

MULLED DRINKS

Spice and sweeten wine, or ale or cider, to suit your own taste and warm the liquid, either directly or by adding hot water until you have a cheering concoction which will hearten as well as warm. Serve in a great punch bowl if you have one or keep warm in a large saucepan or preserving pan on the stove, doling it out with a ladle. If you serve your 'mull' in glasses, put a spoon in first, to prevent cracking the glass. In fact the mull shouldn't really be allowed to get too hot, certainly never to boil, or the flavour will be spoiled.

THE WASSAIL CUP

The wassail cup so widely referred to in prose and poems over the centuries was ale-based, with the addition of cooked apples as well as sugar and spice. In the Epiphany poem by Robert Herrick quoted here it is equated with 'lamb's wooll'.

Next crowne the bowle full
With gentle lamb's wooll
And sugar, nutmeg and ginger,
With store of ale too;
And this you must doe
To make the wassaille a stinger.

Robert Herrick

Carol singers traditionally drank a little from the wassail bowl of each house they visited.

BISHOP'S WINE

Bishop's punch, or 'bischopswyn', is a traditional drink which probably got its name from its association with St Nicholas. The Dutch certainly do drink it on his feast day, 6th December.

1 bottle red wine
1 orange stuck with cloves
cinnamon stick
peel of 1 lemon
sugar to taste

Put the orange and cloves into a large pan and add wine. Leave to steep for half a day to allow them to flavour the wine then add other ingredients and warm for about half an hour before serving.

If you prefer, use 1 bottle sherry or port to 300ml (½ pint) water instead of the red wine.

MULLED CIDER

From the West Country comes this hot sweet cider bowl. Use still cider if you can get it.

1.2 litres (2 pints) cider
2 small eating apples
4 cloves
150 ml (¼ pint) water
55g (2 oz) soft brown sugar
cinnamon stick
5ml (1 teaspoon) ground ginger
1 orange

Bake the apples, stuck with 2 cloves each. Heat the cider. Separately, heat the other ingredients (except orange) until sugar dissolves, then simmer gently for 5 minutes.

Put the baked apples and sliced orange in your punch bowl, strain in the spiced water and pour in the hot cider.

SPICY FRUIT PUNCH

This sort of fruit punch is usually served chilled but there is no reason why a hot version should not be prepared for children or for adults.

600ml (1 pint) orange juice
300ml (½ pint) pineapple juice
600ml (1 pint) water
55-100g (2-4 oz) caster sugar
juice and peel of 1 lemon
½ x 5ml (½ teaspoon)
grated nutmeg
½ x 5ml (½ teaspoon) mixed spice
4 cloves

Heat ingredients gently together until the liquid has absorbed the spice flavours. Decorate with fruit slices if wanted.

Our wassail cup is made
of the rosemary tree,
And so is your beer
of the best barley.
Call up the butler
of this house
Put on his golden ring;
let him bring us up
A glass of beer,
and better we shall sing.

ORANGE GROG

Orange grog is a hot rum-based drink, guaranteed to keep the spirits up on cold winter nights. Grog means any diluted spirit — in this case rum weakened with orange syrup — and is believed to be named after Old Grog, the nickname of an eighteenth-century British admiral who issued rum diluted with water.

3 oranges
300ml (½ pint) water
125g (4 oz) caster sugar
8 x 15ml (8 tbsp) dark rum

Wash the oranges. Pare the rind and then squeeze the juice from two of them and slice the third one thinly.

Put the water into a saucepan with the pared rind and caster sugar and heat gently till the sugar dissolves. Add the orange juice and remove from the heat.

Put 2 x 15ml (2 tbsp) dark rum into each of four heatproof glasses and strain the orange syrup on to the rum. Serve immediately.

HET PINT

Here is a version of the traditional Hogmanay cup of the Scots, somewhat stronger than many Christmassy drinks thanks to the addition of spirits.

1.2 litres (2 pints) mild ale
½ x 5ml (½ teaspoon)
grated nutmeg
55g (2 oz) sugar
2 small eggs, beaten
150ml (¼ pint) Scotch whisky

Heat the ale and nutmeg until almost boiling and then stir in sugar until it dissolves. Add beaten eggs gradually to the pan, stirring continuously to prevent curdling. Add whisky and reheat but don't boil. Pour the whole back and forth until clear then serve.

WHO . . .

1. Thought Christmas was 'humbug'?
2. Used a golden sickle to cut mistletoe from the sacred oak?
3. Wrote *Auld Lang Syne*?
4. Brings gifts to German children on Christmas Eve?
5. Was crowned King of England on Christmas Day 1066?
6. Tried to abolish Christmas altogether in the seventeenth century?
7. Was the author of *The Fir Tree*, a sad Christmas tale?
8. Were Prancer and Vixen, Donner and Blitzen?
9. Did the Romans honour at their midwinter festival?
10. Were the Bold Slasher and the Turkish Knight?
11. Popularized the Christmas tree in Britain?
12. 'Planted' the Glastonbury thorn?
13. Made a life-sized crib scene with real people and animals in Italy?
14. Created the character of Ebenezer Scrooge?
15. Celebrated Kalends in January?
16. Wrote the ode *On the Morning of Christ's Nativity* in 1629?

WHERE . . .

1. Did our Christmas turkey originally come from?
2. Do they celebrate St Lucia's Day on 13th December?
3. Is the New Year gift-giver known as Grandfather Frost?
4. Did Good King Wenceslaus live?
5. Were 'sowens' drunk on New Year's Eve?

A QUIZ FOR CHRISTMAS

6. Does the Kriss Kringle bring gifts at Christmas?
7. Do the Jonkunnu dancers perform at Christmas?
8. Did the characters of Harlequin and Columbine come from?
9. Is the Baddeley Cake eaten on Twelfth Night?
10. Do they eat Stollen at Christmas?
11. Is Up-Helly-Aa celebrated at the end of January?

WHAT . . .

1. Is the popular name for *Crataegus monogyna* 'Biflora'?
2. Country has piñatas for the children at Christmas?
3. Were the Boy Bishops?
4. Is the name of the weeks leading up to Christmas Day?
5. Shape is a French Christmas cake?
6. Were 'the waits'?
7. Pantomime does Buttons traditionally appear in?
8. Is the meaning of 'presepio'?

9. Number of lords are a-leaping in the well-known song?
10. Do the following have in common: chestnuts, oysters, sage and onion?
11. Sort of Christmas food was a 'shrid-pye'?
12. Does 'wassail' really mean?
13. Happens if you find the bean in the Twelfth Night cake?
14. Do glögg and glühwein have in common?
15. Is the popular name for the black hellebore?
16. Were known as 'cosaques' in the 19th century?
17. Were also known as 'guisers'?

WHEN . . .

1. Was the old Christmas Day?
2. Do La Befana, Baboushka and the Tres Reyes Magos bring presents?
3. Was frumenty traditionally eaten?
4. Did King Herod massacre the children of Bethlehem?
5. Are the Christmas decorations traditionally taken down?
6. Does Christmas really begin in both Finland and Poland?
7. Was St Thomas à Becket assassinated?
8. Is Epiphany?
9. Was Het Pint drunk in Scotland?
10. Did people use to go a-corning or a-gooding?

WHICH . . .

1. Roman god is connected with the New Year?
2. Priestly revelry was banned by Henry VIII?

3. People celebrated Juul at midwinter?
4. Wood was used on the fire that first warmed the baby Jesus?
5. Christmas plant was used to kill the god Balder?
6. Three of our favourite carols were composed in the United States?
7. Jewish festival falls in December?
8. Nursery rhyme refers to mince pies?
9. Is the tree most commonly used as a Christmas tree?
10. People held the mistletoe as sacred?
11. English ruler banned the eating of mince pies by Act of Parliament?
12. Traditional entertainment means 'all mime'?
13. Christmas plant was believed to guard against drunkenness?
14. Patron saint of horses has his feast at Christmas time?
15. Common British bird eats mistletoe berries?

ANSWERS

WHO . . .

1. Scrooge in *A Christmas Carol*
2. The Druids
3. The Scots poet Robert Burns
4. The Christkindl
5. William the Conqueror
6. The Puritans in mid-century
7. Hans Christian Andersen
8. Reindeer in Clement C. Moore's poem 'A Visit from Saint Nicholas'.
9. Their god Saturn; it was called Saturnalia
10. Stock characters in the old mumming plays
11. Prince Albert, Queen Victoria's consort
12. Joseph of Arimathaea
13. St Francis of Assisi
14. Charles Dickens
15. The Romans
16. John Milton

WHERE . . .

1. South America
2. Sweden and Finland
3. Russia
4. Bohemia in Czechoslovakia
5. In Scotland
6. In the United States
7. Jamaica
8. The Italian *commedia dell'arte*
9. Drury Lane Theatre, London
10. Germany
11. The Shetland Isles

WHAT . . .

1. The Glastonbury thorn
2. Mexico
3. Young boys who acted as mock-bishops from St Nicholas Day to Childermas (28th December)
4. Advent
5. Log-shaped
6. Carol singers
7. 'Cinderella'
8. A crib
9. Twelve
10. All popular stuffings
11. A mince pie
12. Good health!
13. You are king or queen for the day
14. Both are hot spiced wine drinks
15. The Christmas rose
16. Christmas crackers
17. The mummers

WHEN . . .

1. 6th January
2. At Epiphany
3. On Christmas Eve
4. Holy Innocents' Day, 28th December
5. On Twelfth Night
6. When the first star appears on Christmas Eve
7. Christmas Day 1170.
8. 6th January
9. On New Year's Eve – Hogmanay
10. St Thomas's Day, 21st December

WHICH . . .

1. Janus, whence the name of January
2. The Feast of Fools
3. The Norsemen
4. Ash, because it will burn well while still green
5. Mistletoe
6. 'O Little Town of Bethlehem', 'Away in a Manger', 'We Three Kings'
7. Hanukkah, the Feast of Lights
8. Little Jack Horner
9. Spruce
10. The Druids
11. Oliver Cromwell
12. Pantomime
13. Ivy, the sacred plant of Bacchus
14. St Stephen, 26th December
15. The missel-thrush

A Nativity Play for Children

THIS SIMPLE NATIVITY PLAY CAN BE performed by a cast of seven children, if the Innkeeper doubles as a king, and Herod as a shepherd. If more children are available, the scenes can be expanded – obviously three shepherds are better than two, the Innkeeper should have a wife, Herod a few courtiers, and a heavenly host is always improved by extra angels!

A verse or two of a carol can be sung to ease the change from one scene to the next; some suggestions are included in the text.

The story is told by JOSEPH.

JOSEPH: My name is Joseph. I am a carpenter, and I grew up in a village called Nazareth in Galilee. I was engaged to marry a girl called Mary, but one day something quite extraordinary happened.

MARY: Who are you?

ANGEL: Don't be afraid, Mary. I have been sent by God to bring you some good news. You are going to have a baby son, and he will be called Jesus.

MARY: But how can I have a baby? I'm not even married yet.

ANGEL: No man will be the father of your child. He will be the son of God.

MARY: But that doesn't seem possible.

ANGEL: Your cousin Elizabeth is going to have a child, although everyone thought that she was too old. For God nothing is impossible.

MARY: I know.

ANGEL: Then don't be afraid, Mary. God has chosen you because you are a very special person.

MARY: I am God's servant, and will do whatever he wants.

JOSEPH: When Mary told me what had happened, I didn't believe a word of it. It sounded too incredible. But then the angel visited me as well, and I knew that it was true. Then, just before Mary's baby was due, I heard some news.

MARY: What's the matter, Joseph?

JOSEPH: We have to go to Bethlehem, the town where I was born.

MARY: Why?

JOSEPH: The emperor has ordered everyone to return to their home town to be counted and to be taxed.

MARY: If the emperor has ordered it, then we must go.

JOSEPH: It will be a long, hard journey for you, and we may not get back before the baby is born.

MARY: Don't worry, Joseph. God will look after us.

JOSEPH: So we set off for Bethlehem.

CAROL: *In The Bleak Mid-Winter*

JOSEPH: Bethlehem at last. Now we must find a room at the inn. Hello! Anybody home?

INNKEEPER: Good evening, sir.

JOSEPH: We need a room for the night.

INNKEEPER: I'm sorry, sir, we're completely full up.

JOSEPH: But Mary, my wife, is going to have a baby very soon.

INNKEEPER: I'd help you if I could, sir.

JOSEPH: There must be somewhere we can go.

INNKEEPER: Well, there is always the stable.

JOSEPH: The stable? With all the animals?

INNKEEPER: It will be a roof over your head, sir, and there's plenty of fresh, clean hay.

MARY: That will do very well. Thank you.

JOSEPH: So we stayed that night in the stable, surrounded by all the animals. And there Jesus was born, and Mary wrapped him in swaddling clothes, and for a cradle she used the manger, where the cattle had their food.

CAROL: *Away in a Manger,* or *Once In Royal David's City*

JOSEPH: That night, the local shepherds were out in the fields looking after their sheep, just like any other night. Or so they thought.

SHEPHERD 1: Please don't hurt us.

ANGEL: Don't be afraid.

SHEPHERD 2: Who are you? What do you want?

ANGEL: I am an angel, and I have come from God to bring you some good news. Tonight in Bethlehem a baby was born. His name is Jesus, and he will be a great king.

SHEPHERD 1: Why are you telling us?

SHEPHERD 2: Shouldn't you be telling the important people, like the king and the emperor?

SHEPHERD 1: We are only poor shepherds.

ANGEL: But he too is poor. And this is how you will recognize him. He is in a stable, wrapped in swaddling clothes and lying in a manger. But he will bring glory to God and peace to all men.

JOSEPH: As the shepherds watched, lots more angels appeared, and the sky was filled with songs of praise.

CAROL: *Hark the Herald Angels Sing*

SHEPHERD 1: What shall we do?

SHEPHERD 2: I think we should go to Bethlehem, and find this baby.

SHEPHERD 1: What about the sheep?

SHEPHERD 2: God will look after them.

SHEPHERD 1: Will he?

SHEPHERD 2: Of course. God told us about Jesus before anyone else. He won't let anything harm our sheep.

SHEPHERD 2: We ought to take a present.

SHEPHERD 1: How can we? We haven't got anything.

SHEPHERD 2: We could take him a lamb.

SHEPHERD 1: That's a good idea. Come on then, let's see if we can find this stable.

JOSEPH: When Jesus was born, a great star appeared over Bethlehem, and certain wise men, who knew that it meant the birth of a new king, set out to search for him. After they had travelled many miles they finally arrived in Jerusalem.

CAROL: *We Three Kings*

HEROD: I am King Herod, and I bid you welcome to Jerusalem.

KING 1: Thank you. We are here to look for a baby.

KING 2: A new-born King of the Jews.

HEROD: Why are you looking here?

KING 3: A great new star has appeared in the East.

KING 1: We followed it, and this is where it led.

HEROD: There is no baby here. But the prophets say that the Christ will be born in Bethlehem in Judaea.

KING 2: Then that is where we shall look.

HEROD: And when you find this child, what will you do?

KING 3: We shall offer him the precious gifts that we have brought with us. Gold and frankincense and myrrh.

KING 1: And we shall worship him.

HEROD: Worship a baby? Wise old men like you?

KING 2: Certainly. Because he is Jesus Christ, the Son of God and the Saviour of the World.

KING 3: Greater than any earthly king.

HEROD: I'll tell you what. When you have found him, let me know where he is. Then I can come and worship him too.

KINGS: We will.

HEROD: (*alone*) I don't like the sound of this. There's only room for one king in these parts, and that king is me. When those three let me know where I can find this young upstart, I'll get rid of him. You see if I don't.

JOSEPH: God sent his angel to tell the three wise men what Herod intended, so they knew not to tell him where Jesus was. But they followed the star to the stable, where they presented their precious gifts. And then they joined with the shepherds, and all the animals, and Mary and me in the worship of Jesus, and sang songs of praise, just as we do today.

CAROL: *Oh Come All Ye Faithful*

ALADDIN AND HIS MAGIC LAMP
A Christmas Pantomime for Children

FIRST CHOOSE YOUR STORY – IN THIS case *Aladdin* – and divide it up into its basic scenes, and then work out how many characters you need, or can afford to have (according to the number of willing participants). This *Aladdin* has a cast of seven (six if the Genie of the Lamp doubles as the back legs of the horse!):

WIDOW TWANKEY
ALADDIN, HER SON
HORSE
PRINCESS BADROULBOUDOUR
ABANAZAR, THE VILLAIN
THE GENIE OF THE LAMP

SCENE ONE: IN WHICH WIDOW TWANKEY SETS THE SCENE

WIDOW TWANKEY – *played of course by a man – needs to explain how she, a respectable woman of thoroughly British pedigree, has ended up a penniless washerwoman in Peking. (Though in this Peking you are more likely to find supermarkets and roller skates – not to mention your own Uncle George – than pagodas and rickshaws.)*

WIDOW TWANKEY: Aladdin! Aladdin! Where is that boy? (*Turns and addresses audience*) Hello. I'm Widow Twankey. Fancy meeting you lot here in High Street, Peking. I don't suppose you've seen that layabout son of mine, Aladdin, have you? He told me he was off to the Job Centre to find work. Chance'd be a fine thing. I

know it's not his fault, unemployment being what it is in Peking and him being thick as two short planks. But at least he could lend me a hand sometimes. All I ever get from him is 'What's for supper, Mum?' – and unless I get this washing done there's not going to be any supper. I do all the laundry for the important people here in Peking. By Appointment, I am. Washerwoman to the Gentry. Look at this lot – 23 pairs of socks, 42 thermal vests, 58 pairs of knickers. Here's another one with no name tape on it. How do people expect to get their own knickers back if they don't put their name on them? Oh these ones are marked (*Holds up enormous pair of knickers and names someone in the audience*), and so are these (*Ditto with a pair of long johns*). Ooh, look at these – St Michael. Have to do these extra specially well ... (*And so on.*)

SCENE TWO: IN WHICH ALADDIN INTRODUCES HIMSELF AND HIS HORSE, BEMOANS HIS PENNILESS, JOBLESS AND HUNGRY STATE, AND FIRST ENCOUNTERS AND FALLS IN LOVE WITH THE PRINCESS BADROULBOUDOUR.

A horse is not vital to the plot of ALADDIN, *but all the best pantos have one (unless they have a cow or a goose or a cat instead). All you need is a willing pair of back legs,* prepared to put in a few hours' practice following his front half, and some marvellously comic effects can be achieved. A simple horse's head can be made out of a restructured cardboard box with added ears, but developing a hinged jaw should not present major problems, and a talking — or at least neighing and snorting — horse has infinitely greater potential than a dumb one.

A sympathetic horse would also make an admirable confidante for PRINCESS BADROULBOUDOUR *since pantomime princesses are much given to daydreaming — and if she were to sing a song, the horse could perhaps join in . . .!*

SCENE THREE: IN WHICH THE UNSPEAKABLE ABANAZAR INTRODUCES HIMSELF, DECIDES TO RECRUIT ALADDIN TO HELP HIM RECOVER THE MAGIC LAMP, AND INGRATIATES HIMSELF WITH WIDOW TWANKEY

ABANAZAR'S *introductory speech needs first of all to establish his credentials as an out-and-out villain, deserving to be thoroughly hissed. Threatening the audience is likely to prove unpopular:*

ABANAZAR: I'm Abanazar, and I'm an evil magician. So if you don't watch it I shall fuse the lights on the Christmas tree, I shall make the washing machine overflow and cause a flood, and make the telly go on the blink. And I shall ensure that all the plumbers and electricians are taking a fortnight off for Christmas . . . (*And so on.*)
I had to leave Peking in a hurry. They discovered that it was I who put syrup of figs in the Grand Vizier's sherry, and piranha fish in the emperor's jacuzzi. It was I who caused the fire in the Peking diamond mine, that not only closed an extremely productive pit, but melted the snow on the mountain, closed the ski resort and ruined the tourist industry. Single-handed I ruined the economy, so I'm not very popular with the emperor, and I daren't go back to the mountain. . . .

To hatch his plot, ABANAZAR *needs to eavesdrop on* WIDOW TWANKEY *and* ALADDIN, *and decide to exploit their poverty:*

WIDOW TWANKEY: Stupid boy, mooning around all afternoon with that horse of yours, when there's work to be done.
ALADDIN: What's for supper, mum?
WIDOW TWANKEY: Supper? What are we supposed to buy supper with? We haven't got a bean.
ALADDIN: Mmm. Beans on toast.
WIDOW TWANKEY: There's absolutely nothing in the kitty.
ALADDIN: Poor kitty, she must be as hungry as me.
WIDOW TWANKEY: Ooh, you'll drive me bananas.
ALADDIN: Mmm, bananas and custard.
WIDOW TWANKEY: I shall go crackers.
ALADDIN: Crackers would do, but I'm so hungry I could eat a horse.

WIDOW TWANKEY: That's an idea.

WIDOW TWANKEY *chases the horse, with* ALADDIN *trying to restrain her;* ABANAZAR *intercepts.*

WIDOW TWANKEY: Who are you?
ABANAZAR: Your humble servant, Madam. Who are you?
WIDOW TWANKEY: Everyone knows me. I'm Widow Twankey.
ABANAZAR: Not . . . the widow of the late Mr. Twankey?
WIDOW TWANKEY: The very same.
ABANAZAR: And was he short, fat and bald, with hairy legs?
WIDOW TWANKEY: Certainly not.
ABANAZAR: That proves it. He was my brother.
WIDOW TWANKEY: What?
ABANAZAR: I am your long-lost, very rich brother-in-law, Abanazar.
WIDOW TWANKEY: But I haven't got. . . . Did you say rich?
(*And so on, with* ABANAZAR *buttering up* WIDOW TWANKEY *like mad until she willingly sends* ALADDIN *off with him to the magic mountain.*)

SCENE FOUR: IN WHICH ALADDIN ENTERS THE CAVE, FINDS THE LAMP, BUT REFUSES TO SURRENDER IT TO ABANAZAR, WHO PROMPTLY ENTOMBS HIM IN THE CAVE.

The simplest kind of cave is a large table under which ALADDIN *can crawl, and graphically describe the delights of the interior, while* ABANAZAR *becomes increasingly apoplectic outside, until he finally blows his top and condemns* ALADDIN *to eternal incarceration in the cave. Curses are great fun to write (though beware of the sensibilities of very young children):*

ABANAZAR: Since my wishes you defy,
    Stay in that cave until you die.
    May the air be filled with bats,
    Your toenails nibbled off by rats,
    May you catch a dreadful cough,
    Your ears and fingernails drop off.
    May you wish you weren't alive,
    But live until you're ninety-five . . .

At which point someone should switch off the lights. On this occasion of course it represents the darkness within the cave, but it is quite a good idea to have the lights go
out every time THE GENIE *is scheduled to make an appearance. Not only can* THE GENIE *then appear as an eerily disembodied face by the simple expedient of holding a torch under his chin, but the darkness gives an opportunity to rearrange the scene for the ensuing transformation, in this case to:*

SCENE FIVE: IN WHICH ALADDIN, SAFELY TRANSPORTED HOME AND RECOUNTING HIS ADVENTURES TO WIDOW TWANKEY, DISCOVERS THE TRUE SECRET OF THE LAMP AND ABANAZAR'S VILLAINY IS REVEALED.

Of course, ALADDIN'S *wish is for a magical palace for* THE PRINCESS BADROULBOUDOUR — *and it isn't easy to create a palace, let alone one which flies, in the average family front room. Either an enterprising young artist can paint a large picture, a kind of backdrop which can provide a distant view of the palace — or, as an introduction to the next scene,* THE PRINCESS *can be discovered revelling in her life of luxury with a few select props — a footstool, a huge box of chocolates, a delicate shawl — while she describes the various delights of the palace, and her idyllic life with* ALADDIN.

SCENE SIX: IN WHICH ABANAZAR TRICKS THE PRINCESS INTO GIVING HIM THE LAMP, AND SPIRITS HER AND THE PALACE AWAY TO AFRICA.

The reappearance of ABANAZAR, *albeit disguised in a false moustache, should now automatically trigger loud hissing from the audience, not to mention attempts to warn* THE PRINCESS *with shouts of 'He's behind you!' So* ABANAZAR *will have to work doubly hard at his underhand lamp-salesman act.*

ABANAZAR: Lamps for sale. Lovely brand new lamps for sale, all at factory prices. Standard lamps, neon lamps, headlamps . . .

PRINCESS: Not today, thank you.

ABANAZAR: How about a nice carriage lamp for outside the front door?

PRINCESS: This palace is fully equipped with lamps, thank you very much.

ABANAZAR: I can do you a nice line in chandeliers.

PRINCESS: We have remote controlled spotlights. With dimmer switches.

ABANAZAR: Well, how about this then? I can see you are a woman of taste and refinement, so how about this 100% genuine imitation perfect replica of an ancient Chinese oil lamp?

PRINCESS: Now that's rather nice.

ABANAZAR: Quite the objet d'art, isn't it? Make the perfect Christmas gift for a discerning relative.

PRINCESS: Mm. Perhaps Aladdin would like it.

ABANAZAR: Now you buy one of these in town, it'd cost you £20, but for you, Madam, I'm not asking £5, I'm not even asking £2 . . .

PRINCESS: You see he's got an old one. It's a bit bent and battered . . .

ABANAZAR: I'll accept it in part exchange.

PRINCESS: You will?

ABANAZAR: Tell you what, madam, you give me the old lamp, and I'll not only give you this lovely shiny brand new one in part exchange, I'll throw in this exquisitely carved model of the Eiffel Tower, marked A Present From Peking. . . .

Once ABANAZAR *has got the lamp he has to spirit Palace,* PRINCESS *and all away to the Sahara Desert, which could prove tricky. In the darkness which accompanies* ABANAZAR'S *summoning up of* THE GENIE, THE PRINCESS *will simply have to disappear – along with all her finery – either under the table, or behind the audience, or into another room, where her cries for help can only be faintly heard.*

SCENE SEVEN: IN WHICH ALADDIN, WIDOW TWANKEY AND THE HORSE RETRIEVE THE LAMP FROM ABANAZAR, AND THE PRINCESS AND PALACE FROM THE SAHARA DESERT

The final scene does not require much dialogue beyond:

ALADDIN: Are you going to give me back that lamp?
ABANAZAR: No.
ALADDIN: Oh yes you are.
ABANAZAR: Oh no I'm not. (*And so on.*)

It will take a bit of planning, but a splendid chase could be devised with ALADDIN, WIDOW TWANKEY *and* THE HORSE, *all chasing* ABANAZAR, *but bumping into each other, the back legs of the horse tripping up the wrong people, attempts to ride the horse – and culminating perhaps with* ABANAZAR *being felled with a lethal blow from* WIDOW TWANKEY'S *handbag. A*

final bit of business with the lamp and the genie, the safe recovery of THE PRINCESS, *and we are ready for the final song. Traditionally, this should be copied out on to a huge songsheet, so that someone can point to the words and all the audience sing along. So choose a tune that everybody knows and write some simple words to fit:*

The time has come to say goodbye,
Now isn't that a shame?
This panto's been so wonderful –
Aren't you glad you came?
But Abanazar's on his knees,
Aladdin's won the day,
So we'll just have to end the show –
There's nothing more to say. . . .

Except that all in old Peking
Wish everybody here
A very Happy Christmas
And a Magical New Year.

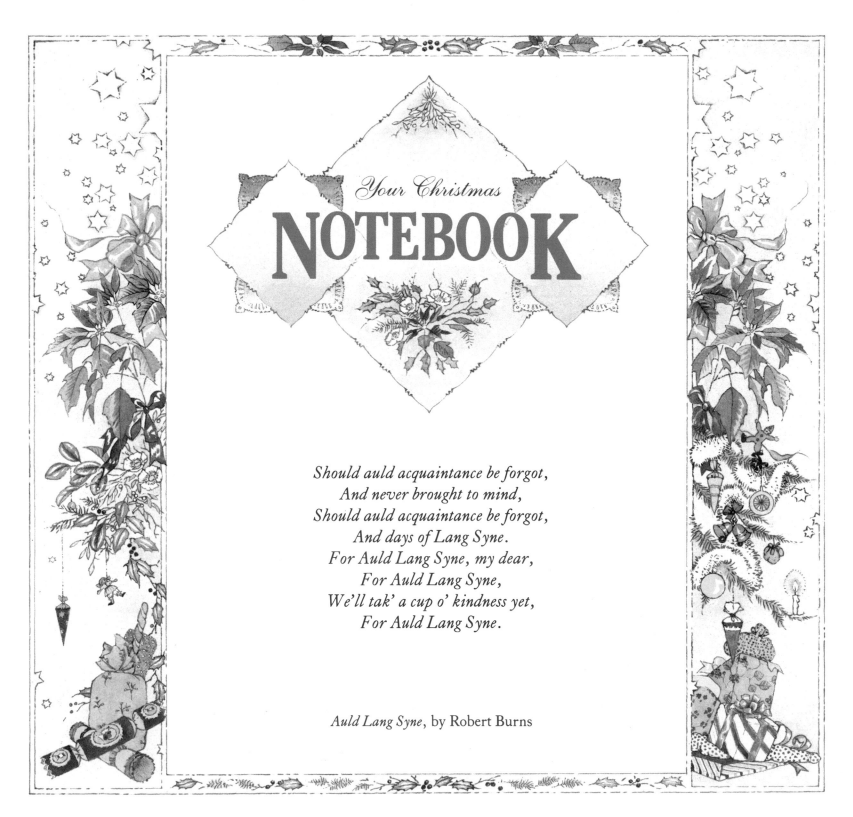

Your Christmas

NOTEBOOK

Should auld acquaintance be forgot,
And never brought to mind,
Should auld acquaintance be forgot,
And days of Lang Syne.
For Auld Lang Syne, my dear,
For Auld Lang Syne,
We'll tak' a cup o' kindness yet,
For Auld Lang Syne.

Auld Lang Syne, by Robert Burns

Christmas
CARDS

Christmas
PRESENTS

Thank-you
LETTERS

ACKNOWLEDGMENTS

Special photography by James Jackson (pages 51, 55, 63, 64, 72, 73) and James Murphy (pages 65 and 69).

Styling by Susie Knight, Penny Mishcon and Christine Parsons.

Illustrations by Heather Jane Davies/ The Garden Studio and Oriol Bath/ David Lewis.

Jacket illustration by Heather Jane Davies/The Garden Studio.

The publishers are grateful to the following for their contribution to this book:

Wendy Rayment, for designing and making the needlepoint stockings shown on pages 50-1.

Angela Fishburn, for writing 'Making your own Christmas Crackers', pages 56-7, and making the crackers shown in the photographs on pages 55 and 73.

Caroline Harrington, for writing the Nativity play, 'Aladdin and his Magic Lamp', and pages 90-5, and the section on pantomimes, page 17.

Pamela Westland, for writing 'Traditional Evergreen Wreaths and Rings', pages 66-7, and 'Evergreen Garlands and Decorations' pages 70-1, and for making the table centrepiece shown in the photograph on page 73.

Details of props used in the special photography:

page 64: mini crystal tree lights by Pifco Ltd; silk flowers by Sia (UK) Ltd.

page 65: mini crystal tree lights by Pifco Ltd; red ribbon from Offray.

page 73: Irish linen place mats and napkins from General Trading Co Ltd; silver-plated 'Du Barry' cutlery by Hugh Fulerton; ribbon by Offray; crystal glasses by Da Vinci; plain white candlelight china by Wedgwood.

The publishers would like to thank the following for their permission to reproduce the photographs in this book:

Aspect Picture Library 24; The Bridgeman Art Library 19 top, 27 right, 42; *Company*/Jan Baldwin 74; Mary Evans Picture Library 1, 4, 6, 8, 12, 14, 15, 17, 18, 19 bottom, 20, 22, 26 left, 27 left, 28, 30, 39, 54, 76, 79, 83; Fine Art Photographic Library 2, 21, 23, 25, 26 right, 36, 96; Mansell Collection 13, 29, 33, 35, 85; Picturepoint 37, 81.

INDEX